OLD TRAFFC

Theatre of Dreams

By:
Iain McCartney

Published by:
Yore Publications
12 The Furrows, Harefield,
Middx. UB9 6AT.

British Library Cataloguing-in-Publication Data.
A catalogue record for this book
is available from the British Library.

ISBN 1 874427 96 8

Printed and bound by Biddles Limited

The Author and Publisher would like to thank
Hilstone Laurie for their help and support .

DEVELOPMENT · CONSTRUCTION CONSULTANTS

Manchester

Paragon House
Seymour Grove
Old Trafford
Manchester M16 OLN

Tel: 0161 877 5177

London

8 Lincoln's Inn Fields
London
WC2A 3BP

Tel: 0171 430 0044

OLD TRAFFORD

THEATRE OF DREAMS

By
Iain McCartney

Iain McCartney - The Author

Iain first visited Old Trafford in the late sixties after following the fortunes of United via Television and the Press. The mid-Seventies saw him become a regular, watching from the Scoreboard Paddock. A decade later he moved to 'G' Stand with a League match ticket book, and still sits there today.

At present he contributes to the United Review, various Supporters Club Newsletters, as well as running the United Collectors Club. To say that United is in his blood is not far off the mark, as he can trace his family tree back to a former captain of Newton Heath.

Acknowledgements:

A special thanks to Tim Laycock, Regional Director with Hilstone Laurie - who have played a major part in the re-development of Old Trafford - for numerous photographs and permission to reproduce same, several of which have been used in this book; also for the special tours of the Stadium that have been arranged. Thanks also to James Thomas for keeping the Author up to date with the goings-on at Old Trafford over the last few years, with the supply of the Manchester Evening News, and to Ole Pedersen of the Scandinavian Branch of the United Supporters Club for help with some of the photographs.

The majority of photographs and other illustrations in this book are believed to be out of copyright, or have been supplied by individuals, with permission to reproduce same. However, despite taking all reasonable steps to avoid infringement of copyright, apologies are offered should this have inadvertently been broken.

Dedication:
To Lynda and Kelly.

✤ CONTENTS ✤

✦ INTRODUCTION ✦

It was still some six hours until kick off time, but the chill of the bright autumn morning could not deter the fans, pilgrims or whatever description is best to describe those congregated around the forecourt of the concrete and metal construction call Old Trafford.

The numbers would begin to increase as the hours and minutes to kick-off time ticked away, but time would not pass quickly enough for some who were making their first trip to the Mecca of English Football. They would stand, oblivious to all around them, consuming every detail, as they long for the red gates at the turnstiles to open and admit them to the arena where they would be swallowed up by the stands of the Old Trafford Stadium. For other, it would be merely a fortnightly ritual, a habit, a love affair, which had begun many years before when they too were brought to the ground for the first time, to watch players from a different era. No matter the outcome of the match, the first trip to Old Trafford will always be remembered. Maybe for a great game, a piece of individual skill, a certain incident, or purely just for being there.

Close your eyes for a moment and imagine the stadium packed to capacity and from the darkened bowels of the old Stretford End, the thespians for today's performance are introduced. It's an all-time United XI which includes the famous names of the past who have graced the hallowed turf....Meredith, Carey, Edwards, Best, Law, Robson, Giggs, Cantona et al.

Welcome to Old Trafford, home of Manchester United Football Club, 'The Theatre of Dreams'.

Old Trafford - June 1996: All development work finished, and ready to stage Euro '96 matches.

✧ IN THE BEGINNING........

To the thousands who flock to Old Trafford on match days, it is difficult for them to imagine the spartan surroundings the club had for homes prior to 1910, and their arrival at the present site.

Newton Heath, as the club began their life in football, had their first home at North Road, Monsall, in the north-eastern Manchester suburb of Newton Heath, close to the carriage and wagon works of the Lancashire and Yorkshire Railway. Hence the original name of the club.

The playing surface of the North Road ground left a lot to be desired, with half the pitch as hard as iron, and the other, soft and muddy. The area surrounding this was little better than a quagmire, and spectators entering the ground at one end needed the footwork of a first class forward to avoid numerous pools of water in the bad weather. During the winter months it was similar heart-rending conditions for both players and followers.

The players had the additional hardship of having no changing facilities at the ground. At first they used the Three Crowns public house on Oldham Road, and later the Shears Hotel, (which also became the club headquarters) some half a mile from the ground. After changing there, they had to walk to and from the ground, with the prospect of a shared bath at the end of their afternoon endeavours.

On October 13th 1892, a record scoreline of 10-1 was recorded against Wolverhampton Wanderers. A report in the Birmingham Daily Gazette mentioned that; *"the pitch was in a terrible state, with pools of water here and there, and Wolves found it difficult to even stand on the muddy pitch"*.

Attendances during that initial season in the Football League were recorded at up to 10,000, and even in those early days the club ranked among the best supported. Those supporters who braved the weather to watch the team, were rewarded with the construction of a stand during season 1891-92, which held 1,000 people.

The ground at North Road belonged to the Manchester Cathedral authorities, but was leased to the club by the Lancashire and Yorkshire railway, who in turn paid a nominal rent to the authorities. There was also a cricket pitch at the site of the ground, and the seasons would overlap, causing problems, with the only solution being a new home for the footballing fraternity. A new company was floated, changing the club name to simply 'Newton Heath', and when the new committee could get little satisfaction from the owners of the North Road ground, a new home became the number one priority.

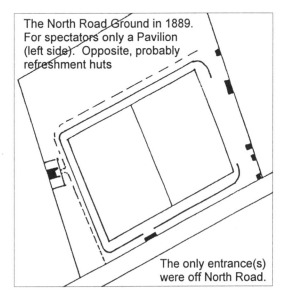

The North Road Ground in 1889. For spectators only a Pavilion (left side). Opposite, probably refreshment huts

The only entrance(s) were off North Road.

Today, North Road has gone, along with the Three Crowns and the Shears Hotel. The whole area has seen wholesale changes since those early days, however, the club still has connections with the area as the present day sponsors, Sharp Electronic, have their home a goal kick from the patch of land that was once the old ground.

So, in 1893, Newton Heath packed whatever belongings they had and moved to a new site, some three miles south, to Bank Lane, Clayton, where a more spacious enclosure was secured. This was let to the club for eight months a year for playing purposes, with pre-season training being allowed to take place on occasional nights.

The new ground was ready for the start of season 1893-94, and had a better playing surface than Newton Heath, but had other distinct disadvantages. It stood beside a chemical works with a background of chimney stacks, which would emit foul smelling fumes, engulfing the players and spectators alike. It was often hinted that if the home side happened to be losing as the match went into its latter stages, workers from the neighbouring works would stoke up the chimneys in an effort to distract the visitors!

Numerous reports during the time at Clayton mentioned the condition at the ground. One, by a gentleman, going under the name of 'Tam' - for the F.A. Cup tie against Chelsea - on February 1st 1908 gave his uninitiated readers an insight into the sometimes atrocious conditions. The scribe wrote of *"thirteen belching chimneys confronting the spectator in the grandstand; where steam in great volumes threatens to envelope the whole place at any moment if the wind but swings round to the west; where the playing pitch is but a bed of grit, though it rolls out as flat and as taking as a running track"*. Another report for a match against Burnley mentioned that the goal posts were so tainted with smoke and dullness of their surroundings as to be hardly discernable.

Ironically, the conditions prevented an entry into the record books, when Walsall Town Swifts were defeated 14-0 on March 9th 1895. The Midland side, however, protested about the terrible ground conditions which clearly favoured the 'Heathens', and after the inquest the match was declared void. On April 3rd, the match was replayed and a 9-0 scoreline showed clearly that it wasn't just the playing conditions that defeated the visitors.

Life at Clayton saw the club finances hit rock bottom, and in 1902 bankruptcy was threatened. Club captain Harry Stafford announced at a shareholders meeting of May 8th that he knew of four people who could put up the £2,000 required to keep the club going. The four were, Mr Taylor of Sale, Mr Brown of Denton, Mr Jones of Manchester and Mr Davies of Old Trafford. It was also suggested that perhaps a change of name would lead to a change of fortune, and after numerous proposals the name of 'Manchester United' was accepted. On April 28th, the Manchester Guardian announced that the club would be known by that name from then on, and a month later the Lancashire F.A. gave formal permission for the name change. And so, a legend was born, and the red and white jerseys which have since become famous all over the world, became the new club colours.

Mr J.H. Davies became the club chairman and president, and although he knew little of the game of football, he made up for this with his business acumen. He was for many years the chairman of the Manchester Brewery, and was a self-made man, living a life of luxury, but never looking down on those less fortunate than himself. Along with his wife, he would travel to watch his club wherever they played, and the players were often invited to his 17th century mansion home at Bramall Hall, where they would be lavishly entertained.

Action at Clayton. United versus Arsenal in the F.A.Cup, 10 March 1906.

The midas touch of John Davies seemed to be rubbing off on the club, as each season saw some improvement, with promotion to the First Division being achieved at the end of season 1905-06 in the runners-up spot.

It had been twelve years since Newton Heath had appeared in the top flight, and now the name of Manchester United appeared in its list of fixtures for the first time. Success continued, and in only the second season back in the big time the championship was won. At last, the loyal band of supporters were getting something to shout about, as the club challenged to be the best.

Although Mr Davies had helped get the club back on its feet and his financial backing had enabled those supporters to enjoy First Division football again, and also taste success, he was very concerned about the conditions at Clayton as he felt that they were an embarrassment to the club. It was not ideal for First Division football, even though a representative match between the Football League and their Scottish counterparts had been played there on April 4th 1904.

John Davies was not a man to rush into things, and certainly did not invest his money in matters where there was no return. In his search for a new site worthy of his beloved United, he scoured the city, before deciding upon a spot to the south-west of the city centre, alongside the Bridgewater Canal, at Old Trafford.

When the decision was made to build a new Ground at Old Trafford, the local railway company, under the name of the 'Cheshire Lines Committee' became heavily involved. One major consideration concerned the viability of building a new Station adjacent to the new stadium. Due thought was given following an objective analysis as to the economic advantage to the railway company. They reasoned that with an anticipated Ground capacity of 100,000, the trains would carry - from central Manchester, five minutes or so away - on average, 10,000 passengers each matchday. With twenty home matches, in addition to proposed athletics meetings on the 'other' Saturdays, and at a return fare of 3d (1½p), this would generate an extra income of £2,750 per annum; a fair return for an anticipated outlay of £9,800 to build a new station. A new road, adjacent to the Railway was also to be constructed, for which the responsibility lay with the Club. The Station was built ('Trafford Park'), but further downline than originally anticipated.

The cost of the ground construction, including the stands, at this time was expected to total about £60,000 - an enormous sum of money in those days.

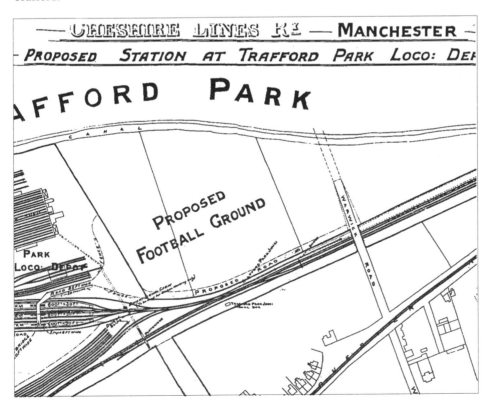

The original outline plans for the Old Trafford Ground - June 1908.

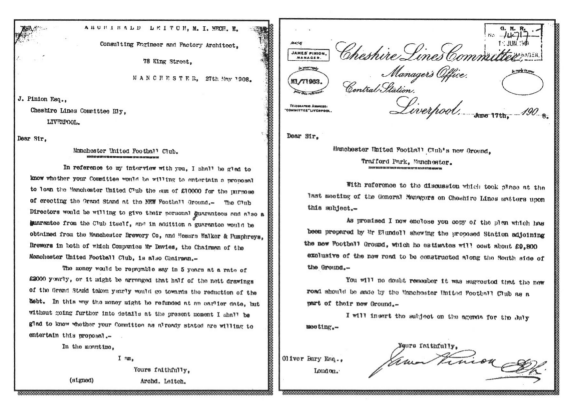

(Above left): The letter from Archibald Leitch (the builder of many Football Grounds), and **(Right)** a letter referring to the proposed station and new road at the new Ground

Archibald Leitch (described as a Consulting Engineer and Factory Architect - despite his Mechanical Engineering qualification), had his offices in Manchester, and was later destined to become the 'father' of football grounds with his many designs, which often incorporated the now famous lattice type decoration on the fronts of the stands. He was responsible for the design of Old Trafford, and it appears that his responsibility extended - at least in part - to raise extra capital needed for the Old Trafford development.

In May 1908, he wrote to the Cheshire Lines Committee with a proposal that they should loan the club £10,000 to fund the building of the Grandstand, which would be paid back at the rate of £2,000 per annum (or alternatively half the gate takings from the Stand until the loan was repaid). Guarantees of the repayment were to be given by the Club directors, the Club itself, and two Breweries - Chairman to both was Mr.Davies, who also held the same post at Manchester United. The proposal received a sympathetic hearing, but, not surprisingly, was turned down.

In the Athletic News dated March 8th 1909 an article entitled 'A Pen Picture Of The Undertaking' by a correspondent called 'Tityrus' described the proposed move to pastures new in great detail, and even today it makes very interesting reading....

"The West of Manchester is destined to be the Mecca of sportsmen of that great commercial city. 'To the west, to the west' will be the cry of our football folks when leaves are falling next autumn. Already we have the Lancashire County Cricket ground, the polo ground, the curling pond, the Manchester Gun Club and numerous other organisations of similar character, devoted to pastime and recreation to the west of the city.

"In September, the Manchester United Football Club will fling open its portals and bid all welcome in the same locality. The contrast between Clayton and the new headquarters of this great football club need not be insisted upon. Clayton is situated in the very heart of the working class community, and dominated on every hand by about forty huge stacks of chimneys belching forth ciminerion smoke

and malodorous fumes. No doubt there are those who feel thankful for a football ground in the vicinity, as it does tend to remind the immediate residents that there is some space left where the toiling people can be amused in a healthy and vigorous manner that pleases them. But an ambitious and a vast club like Manchester United appeals to the 800,000 folks of Manchester and Salford, and an area of larger dimensions, with better accommodation for seeing and housing the spectators and situated in a more attractive locality became essential. Hence the decision of the enterprising directors to lay out an enclosure in the west of Manchester. The new ground lies between the Cheshire Lines railway and the Bridgewater Canal, being a little to the left of the Warwick Road North which juts off the Chester Road. In other words, walking along the Chester Road towards Stretford, one would turn to the south along Warwick Road for the County cricket ground and exactly opposite to the north for the Manchester United football ground.

"The goals in the new arena will be almost west and east, the Stretford goal being the west and the Old Trafford goal to the east. This will give readers an idea of the exact environment in the locality which is expanding. There will not be any difficulty in reaching the new rendezvous. Electric tramcars already run from Clayton to Old Trafford and from the city direct, by two routes. It is proposed to lay down a circular tramway siding just off Chester Road so that the cars can be turned in there, and the passengers having disembarked, the cars can run round the western end of the circle and return to Manchester for more freight.

"There is here a bridge over the Cheshire Lines railway which is to be widened so as to cope with the traffic, while further north on the other side of the ground it is intended to throw a bridge over the canal. But apart from those approaches we understand that the Cheshire Lines committee will open a special station within two or three minutes walk of the western end of this home of sport, so that people can step off the train into the immediate precincts. With such conveniences as these there should never be any difficulty in getter to the place or away from it.

"The Manchester United club have resolved to lay out and equip a huge ground wholly and solely dedicated to football. There will be a running or cycling track around the grass, and for football alone there will not be a better enclosure in England. It is to accommodate 100,000 people and if the greatest matches of the day are not in turn decided to Manchester we shall be surprised, especially as the club is not frightened to expend £30,000 on their undertaking.

"When sightseers cross over the railway bridge, they will find themselves in the midst of a clear space which will serve as a gathering ground 120 feet broad for spectators, and there need not be congestion in gaining access to any portion. With this ground laid out for football alone, the sightseers are brought as near as possible to the playing portion.

"The ground will be rectangle in shape with the corners rounded and it is designed so that everybody will be able to see. The pitch for the game will be excavated to a depth of 9 feet from the ground level so that the boundary or containing wall which is to surround the whole place will only be 30 feet high. There are numerous entrances and spacious exits round the ground. Ingress will be easy and it is estimated that a full ground can be emptied in five minutes.

"Now let us assume that the ordinary spectator has passed through the turnstile. He will find himself in a passage 20 feet broad, which girdles the whole arena. From this, access can be obtained to any portion of the popular terracing, which is virtually divided into three sections. There will be 100 steps of terracing constructed on a special plan, and a nicely judged gradient with of course Leitch's patient crush barriers. The lower portion of this terracing is solid ground, the next higher is formed by the excavated earth and the last and highest is built entirely of ferro-concrete, which is as hard as rock and non-flammable.

"With his practical experience of all the best grounds in these islands, Mr Archibald Leitch M.I.M.E of Manchester who has been the only designer, has endeavoured to cope with these problems. There seems every reason to believe that he has solved it. Now, from this 20 feet passage which will of course afford protection from rain until it is absolutely necessary to go into the arena, the herds of human beings can melt away at will. Right in front of the visitor, whichever entrance they take, will be a flight of very broad but easy stairs, which end in a wide opening or mouth, 60 feet wide and split into three sections.

"The stream of sightseers mounting these stairs and reaching the opening find themselves rather above the middle of the terracing over which they can spread themselves at will. We can picture these great mouths vomiting thousands upon thousands of human beings onto this glorious amphitheatre. The advantage of each mouth is its central position. But if the spectator wishes to go right on top of the terracing, any tier above the sixteenth, he will take another wide staircase which hugs the inside of the boundary wall and lands him on the top of forty tiers of concrete, resting on foundations of the same material, the space underneath being utilised for refreshment rooms and other conveniences.

"Means are provided for transferring from one portion of the ground to another, but it is expected that in a ground devised on this plan, with so many conveniences for reaching the particular position that the spectator desires, there will be little call for transfers, and certainly not to the same extent as on other enclosures.

"The accommodation will, as said, provide for 100,000 people. Of these, 12,000 will be seated in the grandstand and 24,000 standing under steel and slated roofs, so that together there will be room for 36,000 folk under cover and 64,000 in the open, divided between the two arcs of a circle, and the mammoth terracing behind each goal. The roofed part for the populace will be on the southern side and will have open ends with overhanging eaves so that no portion of this erection will obstruct the view of those who are not fortunate enough to secure its shelter on an inclement day.

"The special feature of the grandstand compared with similar erections is that there will not be a paddock in front of it. The spectators will be seated from the barricade round the pitch direct to the back of the stand, in fifty tiers. These fifty tiers are again divided into three sections, the lower, the middle and the highest. Spectators desiring to be comfortable in the grandstand will enter from the turnstiles facing the mouth of Chester Road. They are specially reserved for grandstand visitors only and there they can obtain tickets for any part of the stand.

"Entering there, the spectator will find themselves in a corridor along which run tea rooms, referee apartments, the players facilities, a gym, billiard room and laundry. All of which are to be fitted up in the most modern manner. From this central corridor, there are means of access to the three sections of the grandstand. The lowest or front portion will be approached by a number of passages on the ground floor. To the middle or central portion there are stairs which run practically the whole length of the stand. The highest part is to be gained by means of a distributing passage which is as long as the stand and twenty feet broad. Stairs lead from this to the loftiest section. Thus it will be seen that the structure is designed in such a manner that each person will be able to get to his seat with the least discomfort to himself and the minimum inconvenience to his neighbours, because there is a separate means of ingress to each section of the stand.

"The man who wishes to go to the top of the stand has not to disturb those sitting in the lower rungs and this applies to each portion, for every detail has been carefully thought out, both by Mr Leitch the mastermind and Messrs Bramheld and Smith of Manchester who were responsible for the extensions and improvements at the Clayton ground, the present home of Manchester United F.C.

"The directors, players and officials will obtain access to the field of play from a tunnel which will debouche from the centre of the stand. The offices for the secretary and clerks will be constructed in a portion of the ferro-concrete terracing, almost facing the bridge over the Cheshire Lines. Thus they will be well placed for intending visitors and home officials. Between the grandstand and the railway there will be an enclosed street 45 feet broad, entirely reserved for private motors, not public vehicles.

"Altogether the entire area of the new home of Manchester United will be sixteen acres. The outward circumference of the ground will be about 2000 feet. The ground will be 630 feet long and

510 feet broad, the width of all the terracing being 120 feet. This is a palatial ground which will challenge comparison with any in Great Britain. The executives of the club are to be congratulated on their spirited policy which no doubt will be met with reward from the football public".

For those familiar with the ground up until the early sixties, it is not difficult to visualize the plans for the stadium in those bygone days. However, before finalising the plans, Mr J.J. Bentley, the club secretary, suggested several refinements, such as the cycle track and reducing the height of the terracing. Although this reduced the proposed capacity, it did in fact cut the costs to around £60,000.

The plans for the new stadium were approved by the Stretford District Council on March 2nd, with conditions such as the widening of Warwick Road and the railway bridge to be carried out at the same time. While the plans for Old Trafford were being transferred from paper to concrete and cement, Clayton continued to be used as the club's home, and remained so up until January 1910, when Tottenham Hotspur became the last League visitors to the witches cauldron of Bank Street, on the 22nd of that month.

A crowd of around 5,000 turned up to say their goodbyes, (a far cry from the twenty to thirty thousand that used to pack inside), as United required little help from their 'magic smells', to win comfortably 5-0. The reserve team continued to use the ground for a further two years, until the lease ran out on January 1st 1912

It is perhaps just as well that the Tottenham game was the last senior fixture played there, as a few days later the stands were blown down during a severe storm which caused quite a bit of damage in the Clayton area as well as at the old home.

Bank Street still remains, and for a time the area was dominated by a huge power station just behind the site of the ground, which is still visible. The air continues to be thick with the smoke from nearby industry, but no doubt in years to come Bank Street will become but a memory as one change makes way for another. It is, however, difficult to imagine that such a location was once the home of Manchester United.

(Above) The lease for the 1909-10 season at Bank Street (at £220 per annum)

(Left) The damage at the Bank Street ground caused by the storm, in January 1910.

✧ OLD TRAFFORD: 1910 - 1945 ✧

1910: An Artist's impression of Old Trafford, from the (later) scoreboard end. The Stand on the right was never built

---

Manchester United Football Club. Ltd.

WINNERS OF THE LEAGUE CHAMPIONSHIP, 1907-8.
WINNERS OF THE MANCHESTER CUP, 1908.
WINNERS OF THE FOOTBALL ASSOCIATION CHARITY SHIELD, 1908.
WINNERS OF THE ENGLISH CUP, 1909.

TELEPHONE 68, OPENSHAW.   BANK STREET, CLAYTON
TELEGRAMS:
MANGNALL, CLAYTON, MANCHESTER."   MANCHESTER.
SECRETARY:
J. E. MANGNALL.   *February 15th, 1910.*

OPENING OF NEW GROUND,

Manchester United v. Liverpool,

FEBRUARY 19th. 1910.

Dear Sir,

The President (Mr. J. H. Davies) and Directors of the Manchester United Club ask your acceptance of enclosed, and extend a cordial invitation to attend the opening Match on Saturday next.

The ground is situate at Old Trafford near the County Cricket Ground, and can be reached by three tram routes—Deansgate, Piccadilly and St. Peter's Square.

The ground when completed will hold over 100,000 people. The present Stand will accommodate 12,000 people seated.

An early reply will greatly oblige.

Yours truly,

J. E. MANGNALL.

Secretary.

So, it was Manchester United Football Club of Old Trafford from now on, and it was all systems go to have the new stadium ready for the visit of Lancashire neighbours Liverpool, on Saturday February 19th 1910, for the inaugural match. This should really have been the second fixture at Old Trafford, with the visit of Tottenham Hotspur on January 22nd scheduled for the opening. However, with the work on the ground not yet complete the supporters had to wait just a little longer to meander through the cobbled streets to their new home ground.

Traffic was particularly heavy in the Stretford area on the day of the Liverpool match, as all imaginable forms of transport headed towards Old Trafford, with those not fortunate enough to own, be able to pay for or be offered a lift on a vehicle of some sort, making their way on foot. Admission was 6d(2½p) for the ground and 1/-(5p), 1/6d(7½p) and 2/-(10p) for the covered stand. There were also a few reserved seats in the centre of the stand at 5/-(25p).

The surroundings were something of a dream world for the 50,000 present, but they were soon brought back down to earth with a bump as the visitors won 4-3, fighting back from 2-0 down.

As kick-off time approached, it was not easy to estimate the attendance inside, but around the ground and on the approach roads it was quite obvious that both the gatemen at the turnstiles and the Manchester Tramways were having difficulty in coping with the vast crowds. Today's record books give the attendance at 45,000, but it is believed that some 5,000 more managed to gain illegal entry by various means, including a small unfinished window fanlight.

So, the lush green turf with its vivid white line markings looked immaculate as the sun shone down on it, with the red and white quartered corner flags fluttering in the afternoon breeze. Within fifteen minutes of the start, a diving header from Sandy Turnbull, following a Duckworth free kick, and Homer, following through a Halse shot which the Liverpool goalkeeper could only parry, had given United a 2-0 lead. The visitors began to regain some of the play and soon pulled a goal back, but the two goal advantage was soon re-established when Wall scored with an oblique shot from the left wing.

The white shirted Liverpool players refused to give in, and their resilience was rewarded as they began to get the better of the United defence. Goddard soon made it 3-2, Stewart equalised and then scored what was to be the winner near the end as rain began to fall on the subdued spectators. Not the best of starts, but with the surroundings as unfamiliar to United as they were to Liverpool it was not what could be considered as a shock defeat.

So, with the initial fixture out of the way, things could only become easier in the day to day running of the club at its new home.

Within months of the ground coming into use, United were honoured by the Football Association, who asked the club to stage the 1910 F.A. Cup Semi-Final tie between Barnsley and Everton, while a year later, 56,607 packed into the ground, paying £3,487 to watch Bradford City face Newcastle United in the F.A. Cup Final replay. These events were soon to become a common addition to the Old Trafford fixture list, with eight semi-finals and two Final replays being played there prior to the Second World War. Such games also provided an extra source of income for which the club were always grateful, although financial problems were not something which caused the management of the time any sleepless nights, with £12,000 of the ground debt paid of in 1912 and plans for further development well advanced.

Every consideration was being given to the supporters, and the attracting of new support, that a bridge was to be built to give easier access to Salford and a large car shed was to be constructed close to the stadium for Salford cars.

On April 2nd 1915, five years after the opening of the stadium, United played what was to be their most talked about fixture to date, ironically Liverpool were again the opposition.

On the morning of the match, F.A. representatives, Mr Frederick Wall and Mr Arthur Kingscott, visited the ground to discuss arrangements for the forthcoming F.A. Cup Final, on April 24th, to be played at Old Trafford. It was rather fortunate that they had to leave prior to the kick-off, as the events of that particular afternoon produced much debate in the days and weeks ahead. On a pouring wet afternoon, the 15,000 crowd endured more than adverse weather conditions, but also a performance by both teams which contained some very dubious play.

United began quite promisingly, and indeed opened the scoring with a goal from Anderson. Liverpool, however, were expected to take both points, as United were not having the best of seasons, sitting in a precarious position, third from bottom of the table with only eight games remaining and a place in Division Two beckoning.

But, as the first half progressed, the visitors showed little appetite for the game and play sluggishly dragged on to the interval. Half time opinion suggested that the second forty-five minutes would see the home side up against it as their Lancashire neighbours committed themselves more to attack and began to show their true form. As it turned out, this was not to be the case, and it soon became obvious to a large majority of the crowd that they were witnessing something a little more involved than a simple game of football, and voices of displeasure soon began to echo around the ground.

Play continued to be rather mundane, until a United attack on the visitors goal saw a Liverpool defender being penalised and a penalty kick was awarded. To the crowd's amazement, centre half O'Connel stepped up to take the kick instead of the regular penalty taker Anderson, the scorer of the first goal. O'Connel's effort gave the goalkeeper no cause for concern and flew well wide of the post.

Anderson eventually did secure the points for United with his second goal, although near the end

Liverpool's Pagnam almost pulled a goal back, but his shot rebounded off the crossbar. For his effort, he received a severe reprimand from some of his teammates, as the crowd looked on in disbelief.

Two valuable points for United, but the press were not lacking in comment on the fixture - *"the most uninteresting game ever seen at the ground"* wrote the Sporting Chronicle, with the Daily Dispatch writing *"United's West was clearly employed in the second half in kicking the ball as far out of play as he could"*.

A couple of weeks after the match, a letter appeared in the Sporting Chronicle signed 'Football King', on behalf of a firm of bookmakers asking if anyone could help with information relating to several players betting on the United - Liverpool match ending in a 2-0 win for the home side? This opened a can of worms, and although the finger of suspicion was pointed at several United players, they managed to keep their minds on playing and relegation was avoided.

In the meantime, a committee was assembled by the Football League to investigate the allegations arising from the match and the referee, John Sharpe, was even quoted as saying that following the penalty he *"suspected that something was amiss"*, but decided to continue although it was the most extraordinary match he had ever officiated over. United manager, Jack Robson, was also disgusted by the performance and had left the ground before the final whistle. Following many hours of questioning players from both side, the investigating committee announced that four Liverpool players, along with A.Turnbull, Whalley and West of United were to be suspended sine-die from football.

Much was made of the case, and "Knocker" West went to great lengths to declare his innocence in the matter. So incensed was he that he decided to take the matter to court. Prior to a home fixture during the First World War, he stood outside Old Trafford handing out leaflets which stated he was prepared to give £50 to any Red Cross Fund if anyone could prove that he had placed a bet, or won any money, from the Good Friday fixture. No one came forward.

On July 5th 1917, some two years after the eventful confrontation, the court case opened, and while some players denied all knowledge of any attempts to fix the game, others, including Sheldon

of Liverpool (a former United player) suggested otherwise. It was revealed, that on the morning of the match he had journeyed to Manchester alone, meeting up with former United teammates Turnbull, Whalley and West, in the Dog and Partridge pub close to Old Trafford. After much conversation, it was agreed that the result of the game would be 2-0 to United, with a goal in each half. Sheldon had been approached previously and had made arrangements with some of his Liverpool teammates regarding fixing the result, and how everything was finalised.

Following the First World War, when American servicemen had used the Old Trafford pitch for baseball, it took a while for life to return to normal as the hostilities had effected everyone, but slowly recreational activities began to regain importance and football was soon to enjoy an increase in attendance figures.

Some 258,000 spectators attended the eleven First Division fixtures on the opening day of season 1919-20, the first after the war. It was soon to prove a boom time for the vast majority of clubs, United included, as the turnstiles clicked merrily away on match days. On December 27th 1920, however, they were put into overdrive as some 70,500 passed through the gates (with thousands locked out), paying £4,824 to watch United play Aston Villa. One newspaper at the time gave a different figure - 72,000, but this was not regarded as official and the lower figure is that which appears in the record books today. It was certainly a busy festive period for the turnstile operators as the previous day, 15,000 had been at the ground to watch a reserve fixture between the two clubs, which ended 0-0. That same afternoon, United won a seven goal thriller at Villa Park 4-3, but their supporters were to be disappointed in that Old Trafford return match as Villa won 3-1.

The visitors had taken a two goal lead, with United failing to make the most of their chances, although they did hit the crossbar on a couple of occasions. Harrison managed to pull one back, but Villa took everything in their stride and soon added a third. The following day, United played yet another match, against Corinthians, in a friendly, but this only attracted a mere 3,000.

Towards the end of that 1920-21 season another record attendance was set, when a crowd of 13 paid to watch Stockport County play Leicester City in a Second Division match.

Stockport's ground was closed by the Football Association at the time, hence the reason for their appearance at Old Trafford. The attendance is, however, a little misleading, as the game was watched by quite a lot more, as United had been at home that same day to Derby County, and some of the 10,000 remained inside the stadium at full-time to watch a second game free.

The ground record attendance did not last for long, as the previously estimated attendance of 72,000 became a reality on March 24th 1923, when Bolton Wanderers faced Sheffield United in an F.A. Cup semi-final, bringing in gate receipts of £7,600. By 2pm, the gates were firmly locked, with thousands still milling around outside the ground. One Sheffield United supporter rushing towards the turnstiles passed a friend and enquired which way he was going. *"Home"* came the unexpected reply. Inside the ground, the scene was remarkable, with the popular side (now United Road) a mass of heaving, swaying bodies moving in all directions like a human tide. Many were squashed against the barriers, while for others the heat was too much to bear and having fainted, they were passed over the heads of their fellow supporters to the sanctuary of the touchline.

Along the touchline on other parts of the ground were spectators who had suffered similar feelings, but who had been forced bodily across the fencing at the front. The police tried in desperation to force them back but to no avail, and many watched the game from a more comfortable spot near to the touchline. When all was considered, it was perhaps a little surprising that the game went ahead as scheduled.

Sadly, the match itself couldn't compare to the pre-match excitement and was cautiously played with neither side prepared to take any chances. Bolton, perhaps, just deserved to win and move on to become one of the finalists in the first ever Wembley final, and many of their enthusiastic supporters invaded the pitch at full- time to carry their heroes off shoulder high.

The following year, 1924, produced a couple of interesting occasions in the history of Old Trafford, with United involved in neither. February saw the ground become a guinea pig for an experiment which would later become a compulsion with thousands of people from all walks of like, and not just followers of football. John Moores, who later became chairman of Everton and was at one point listed as the second richest man in Britain, had picked up the idea of 'football pools' from a failed Birmingham entrepreneur and had persuaded two friends to put up £30 each for the first batch of coupons. Those coupons were then taken to Old Trafford where Moores hired some children to hand them out to supporters attending a match. Much to his dismay, the idea was not an immediate success as only 35 out of 4,000 were returned. This, however, was a much better return than that of a future attempt at Hull, when only 1 from 10,000 was returned!

The second 'first' was a few months later when Lancashire County hired the stadium to play the New Zealand All Blacks at rugby, with United receiving 20% of the gross gate.

A year after that debut appearance of the football coupon came another surprising debut and this time United were very much involved. On February 7th, Clapton Orient journeyed north to play a Second Division fixture and shortly after arriving at the ground they found themselves involved in transfer negotiations with United wanting to sign their centre forward Albert Pape. The player, and both clubs, agreed to the transfer details, the move was approved by the Football League over the telephone, and Pape lined up against his colleagues with whom he had travelled north. He also managed to get his name on the scoresheet, scoring United's fourth in a 4-2 win.

Old Trafford must have formed a favourable impression with the Football Association, because on April 17th 1926, the 'Auld Enemy' - England and Scotland - graced the Old Trafford turf for its inaugural International fixture, in what was the 50th meeting between the two countries. The occasion brought out of the best in Manchester United, with the ground in immaculate condition and the production of an excellent 12 page programme. Allied Newspapers, with the authority of the United directors, also published a souvenir of the occasion in the form of a 112 page brochure which contained a history of the club, with details for various players and containing numerous photographs.

As for the game itself, it certainly matched the atmosphere with some 10,000 Scotsmen creating more noise than the rest of the 40,000 present. Prior to the kick off a number of the visiting scots invaded the pitch to embrace their favourites, and again at the end their enthusiasm got the better of

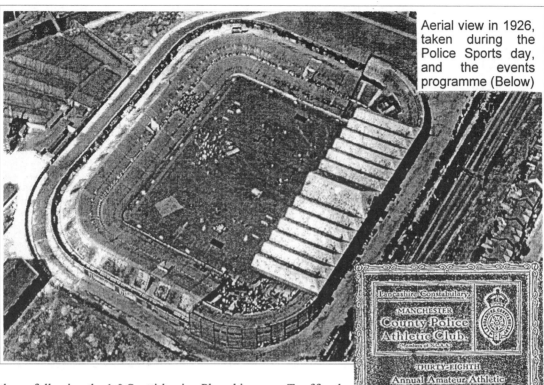

Aerial view in 1926, taken during the Police Sports day, and the events programme (Below)

them, following the 1-0 Scottish win. Played in a friendly, but competitive, spirit with good control from the referee, the individuality of the Scottish team shone through. The only goal of the game came from Jackson, following a move between that same player and Hughie Gallagher, with a shot going in off the post.

During the summer months, most football stadiums are deserted places, with repair and maintenance work the only action being undertaken. However, the summer of 1927 saw a week of activity with Mr C.B. Cochran hiring Old Trafford for "Exhibition Tennis by Madame Lengle". Suzanne Lengle was a Wimbledon champion, but compared to Joe Spence and Co. she was a minor attraction and attendances were disappointing.

Since the early 1920's United's financial situation had somewhat improved and the overdraft at the bank was reduced from £3,355 to zero, by season 1926-27. Attendances had increased with the return of First Division football in 1925, a derby match against City attracting 48,657, while a 5th round F.A. Cup replay against Sunderland was watched by 58,661 paying £4,823. Everything looked rosy and the board of directors decided, after much debate, to purchase the freehold of Old

Trafford, which at that time was costing £1,300 per year in rent and rates. The Manchester Brewery Co. agreed to the proposal as contained in the original contract and on March 25th 1927 all was completed. Shortly after this, the club's benefactor since 1902, Mr J.H. Davies, died leaving something of a void at the club. His presence and expertise was soon to be missed as United began to struggle on the field of play.

Season 1930-31 was nothing short of disastrous, with every one of the opening twelve fixtures being lost. Attendances dropped from 18,004 on the opening day against Aston Villa to 10,907 for the third home fixture against Newcastle United. Scorelines such as 6-2, 6-0 and 7-4 were not tolerated by the support and it was soon obvious to everyone that frustration was mounting.

Leaflets were handed out by members of the supporters club with many opinions put forward to the cause of the poor start, but the directors chose to keep their heads in the sand.

By mid-October, things were reaching boiling point and following the 5-1 defeat at West Ham, the supporters club called a meeting at Hulme Town Hall on the Friday night prior to the home fixture against Arsenal on the 18th, with plans afoot to boycott the match. Some 3,000 attended the meeting, and the board were unanimously give a vote of no confidence, with Mr Greenhough, the supporters club secretary, proposing that the match the following should be boycotted. Former United captain, Charlie Roberts, was at the meeting since he was the man the supporters club wanted to put on the board as their representative, and he spoke out against such an idea, but a show of hands saw his opinion waved aside.

So, armed with his soap box, Mr Greenhough set off for Old Trafford on Saturday October 18th, hoping that the feelings of the meeting the previous night would be carried over and the board would pay attention to the most important people behind the club - its supporters. Extra police were on duty to quell any unruly behaviour, but heavy rain seemed to dampen the spirits a little, and the intended boycott was reported in the press as a failure due to the attendance of 23,406, which was not only the highlight of the season so far, but the highlight for the entire season, except for the Manchester 'derby'.

Many had travelled to the ground to view the pre-match events, expecting some excitement, and after listening to what Mr Greenhough had to say, they paid their money at the turnstiles and watched the game, which United lost 2-1.

It is worth noting, that Mr Greenhough was not some trouble-seeker or self-centred individual, but a fervent United supporter. He was one of the initial forces behind the formation of the first supporters club in the mid 1920's and along with his fellow committee members and other willing hands, swept the ground each week and helped in its maintenance. The Supporters Club, whose headquarters was at the Clowes Hotel, Trafford Road, Salford, also had a hut on what was the United Road side of the ground where they catered for the spectators on match days with various refreshments. The hut was also used on Sunday mornings, when members and players met to discuss the game the previous day and also to play cards, darts etc.

Rain again poured down on Manchester when United finally recorded their first victory of the season, 2-0 against Birmingham City in front of 11,479, but this was not the beginning of any improvement.

The 1930's were a troubled time for everyone, with rising unemployment and a lack of ready cash a worry for businesses and individuals alike.

Old Trafford in the 1930's

It was no different for United, who had to approach the Brewery Co. and ask for their mortgage interest payments to be suspended along with a similar application to the Stretford

Urban District Council for permission to pay road charges by instalments. With financial problems mounting at the Bank, a solution had to be found or the club would find themselves in serious trouble. Thankfully, help did arrive, in the form of Mr J.W. Gibson who immediately set about reorganising the club affairs.

Rumours that United were to move away from

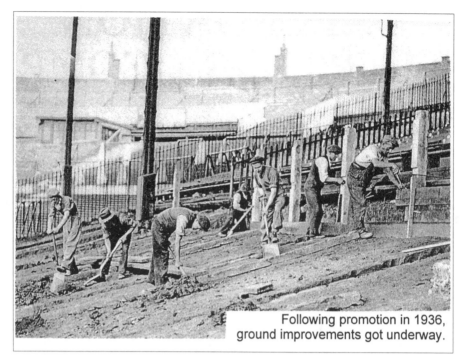

Following promotion in 1936, ground improvements got underway.

Old Trafford were in circulation in 1932, but were firmly scorched when plans were made and carried forward, to cover the popular side of the ground. Relegation to Division Three in 1934 would have been a nightmare for the club, but they managed to survive by the skin of their teeth and things could only improve.

Through these depressing times, Old Trafford was still one of the finest grounds in the country. Prior to season 1938-39 the wing terraces had been roofed giving cover to some 4,000 spectators, while beneath the main stand, a new treatment room was set up along with a cobblers shop. The dressing rooms were also decorated, bringing in bills for some £35,000. Such improvements kept the ground in contention to hold 'big events' such as F.A. Cup semi-finals, while November 1938 saw the Football League entertain the Irish League.

The English eleven turned on a memorable display, with Stanley Matthews at his masterly best, teasing and tormenting the Irish defence, and helping to provide Tottenham's Willie Hall with five goals in a 7-0 victory. Three of those goals came in a five minute spell, all provided by Matthews and it was fitting that the man from the Potteries rounded off a fine afternoons work by completing the rout with a fine solo goal.

Towards the end of season 1938-39, the F.A. awarded Old Trafford yet another semi-final tie, with Wolves Vs Grimsby Town playing there on March 25th. A recorded 76,962 squeezed into the stadium to watch the tie - paying £8,193 - and created two new ground records. The Midlands side won 5-0, but the scoreline was a little misleading as they were not as superior as it suggests.

August, to football followers, is the month of the year which heralds the start of a new season, with dreams of honours and excitement in the months ahead. 1939, however, was very much different, with the outbreak of the Second World War imminent and the whole country was on a state of war footing. The Football League decided to keep things as they were and prepared complete fixture lists for all divisions, despite the general unrest and the possibility of what might lie ahead.

Old Trafford was the venue for only one League fixture before hostilities got under way, with a crowd of around 20,000 present to watch United beat Grimsby Town 4-0, on August 26th. On September 3rd, war was declared, (with only three fixtures having been completed), and Old Trafford was requisitioned as a temporary depot for the military, with the Cliff training ground (purchased a few years earlier) being used by the R.A.F.

The government at first ordered clubs to refrain from playing, due to the threat of ariel attacks, but later did an about-turn as they felt that any form of recreation would help boost the moral of the people and transfer their thoughts to something else for a short period of time The Football League was disbanded and Divisional Leagues set up, with United in a Western Division made up of northern clubs. Attendances were usually around 8,000, which was the restricted level, but in the summer Cup competition at the end of the season, such restrictions were lifted to enable 40,000 to watch United face City. However, only 21,874 turned up for the first leg of the tie.

By the summer of 1940, Britain was more involved in the war, due to the capitulation of France in July. The Football League, however, decided to continue with fixtures for the forthcoming season. Christmas day 1940 should have seen Stockport County visit Old Trafford for a North Regional League match, but on the night of Sunday December 22nd, German aircraft bombed Trafford Park. During the air raids over 300 Mancunians were killed and Old Trafford was damaged.

The Stockport match was switched to County's ground and the following fixture, three days later against Blackburn Rovers, was also played at Stockport.

Old Trafford was tidied up, and fixtures were resumed in the Lancs. Cup and League War Cup. The North Regional League fixtures resumed on March 8th with a match against Bury, when hat-tricks from Rowley and Carey, along with a single Smith goal, thrilled a 3,000 crowd in a 7-3 win. This, however, was to be the last competitive match to be played at Old Trafford until 1949. The night of March 11th saw another German bomb attack on Manchester, this time causing much more damage and devastation, with the ground and nearby Trafford Park again suffering badly.

So, on the 556th day of the war, United lost most of the main stand, dressing rooms and offices. Temporary accommodation was made available at Cornbrook Cold Stores, owned by chairman Mr J.W. Gibson, where club affairs were continued by secretary Walter Crickmere.

United were now homeless, and while arrangements were being made with the Stretford Corporation to dismantle what was left of the stand and salvage the steel, along with demolishing other unsafe parts of the ground, claims for war damage to property were put forward to the authorities.

Neighbours City offered their unfortunate rivals a helping hand, with the use of their Maine Road ground until the time when Old Trafford was in a playable condition again. It was a lifeline United needed, and grasped thankfully, as they were determined to continue with their fixtures as best they could. Following clearance from the Football League, Maine Road became home for both the Blue and the Red factions of Manchester. The war continued to dominate everyone's life and United were content to continue as City's lodgers, with Old Trafford remaining unkept and dormant several miles away. City were also grateful for the extra revenue, received in rent from United.

On November 17th 1944 the War Commission wrote to the club directors to say the Old Trafford was *"not considered a total loss"*, but it was still some time before any repair work could be proposed. Local MP Ellis Smith, a keen United supporter, became very much involved in the club's attempts at obtaining grants towards the rebuilding of the ground and this involvement continued for many years after the war ended in 1945.

Old Trafford after enemy bombing had taken its toll

So, with war in Europe finally over, servicemen were returning home while throughout the country attempts were being made to try and regain some form of normality. United, however, found themselves in a situation similar to that of days gone by - a ground in much need of repair, debts of large sums of money, and no manager. One third of the problem was solved on Monday February 19th 1945, when former Manchester City and Liverpool wing-half Matt Busby was appointed manager. Standing on the rubble strewn terraces looking around the deserted stadium with a large bush growing on the pitch, what thoughts penetrated his mind?

In August of that year, the War Damage Commission granted the club a sum of £4,800 to clear the debris around the ground, with a further £17,478 towards the rebuilding of the stands. The payments, were made by instalments, with the final sum (£710-14-0) for the demolition work not being paid until February 1947.

By April, the difficult job of pulling down the entire stand and the wall behind it was completed, leaving an open space along with some foundations. During the summer, the wall was rebuilt and dressing rooms were erected, with repair work on the covered section on the opposite side of the ground carried out. The playing surface, although in good condition, was to be given 300 tons of special soil and new turf was laid down the centre from one goal to the other.

United had hoped to kick off season 1946-47 back in familiar surroundings instead of the shared accommodation at Maine Road, but the club accounts for season 1945-46 mentioned that owing to the persistent acute shortage of building materials it had not been possible to reinstate the club premises and they would continue to use City's ground. Some 30,000 did squeeze into the ground in early August to watch a Reds Vs Blues practise match which ended in a 3-3 draw, and both United and City reserves played their Central League fixtures there, but the serious business of League football was played a few miles away.

In the opening 'United Review' for 1946-47, Chairman Mr J.W. Gibson wrote...

"A lump rises in my throat when I think of our premises at Old Trafford damaged beyond repair by fire and blast in March 1941 and still looking a sorry spectacle owing to government policy of issuing only limited licences for building materials whilst the housing problem is so manifest."

By December, plans had been drawn up for the proposed 'new look' Old Trafford once permission was given. The architects drawing gave the impression of large covered stands, spacious terracing accompanied by up-to-date facilities for the players. It was hoped that the capacity could rise to around 125,000 with the railway station alongside the ground providing quick and easy access to and from it. Could the ideas on paper be transferred into brick and concrete?

With City enjoying the extra income from the attendances that United attracted at Maine Road, the reserve team fixtures at Old Trafford never produced 'ground full' notices or anywhere near it. However, on June 6th 1947, the Old Trafford gates were firmly locked with 36,000 inside, having purchased their tickets weeks before, to watch Salford Schools play Leicester Schools in the English Schools F.A. Final replay. The Salford schools had been more than happy with their 0-0 draw against the current holders in the first match, but a venue for the replay did cause a problem. Earlier round ties had been played at the Cliff, but such was the interest in the Final, a larger venue was required. After consultation with the local constabulary, a 36,000 all-ticket limit was put on Old Trafford and a strong police presence was prominent at the ground to prevent spectators encroaching on the bomb damaged areas.

It had been a long time since vocal encouragement similar to that given to the Salford lads had been heard in the vicinity, and the youngsters provided excellent entertainment. The crowd certainly received their moneys-worth as the match went into extra-time with neither side having scored after ninety minutes. In extra-time, the local boys soon made the breakthrough and went on to add a second, to lift the trophy for the first time.

Salford schools were not the only people who wanted to use the bomb damaged Old Trafford as a look through the directors weekly meeting

minutes show, with names such as the Cheshire Association, Manchester Youth Organisation League, Manchester Schools, and Christies Hospital all writing for permission to use the humble facilities.

November 1948 saw City give United notice to quit Maine Road, as they were beginning to find it somewhat restricted with both clubs continued sharing of the ground. This helped United push forward their plans for the further improvement of their own stadium as they were becoming a little exasperated with the limited progress made, having hoped originally to have been in full operation again in the previous season. As the end of 1948 approached, the efforts towards ground improvements increased, and one supporter, a Mr H.S. Thompson from Stockport, went as far as organising a petition with the hope of persuading the Ministry Of Works to expedite the issue of licences for the restoration of Old Trafford. Mr Thompson had already approached Members of Parliament and had between 200 and 300 fellow supporters standing by ready to help with any work involved at the ground.

PETITION

TO THE MINISTRY OF WORKS

Appealing for the necessary permits and licences to restore the accommodation at

MANCHESTER UNITED FOOTBALL CLUB GROUND

Old Trafford, which was destroyed by enemy action during the last war. This is our only form of recreation to which we look forward after a week's hard work & we, the undersigned spectators, hereby appeal to you for your consideration

ORGANISER To whom all forms should be returned H. S. THOMPSON, 58 WELLINGTON ROAD SOUTH, STOCKPORT.

The supporters urged the authorities to help them to return 'home'.

By the end of April 1949, the final remnants of war damage had been removed and the levelling and concreting of the stand area begun. A section was made into the concrete terracing and some cinema type seats procured to accommodate around 3,000, all without cover. But who would care, being back home would be enough. Cover was provided, however, for the directors and press, with a corrugated iron awning constructed over their respective boxes in an attempt to keep out any inclement weather. So, at 6.30pm on Wednesday August 24th 1949, United ran out onto the Old Trafford lush green turf for the first League fixture there since 1939, to face neighbours Bolton Wanderers.

(Left) the first match back - the public practise match, and (right) the Bolton Wanderers programme.

In the club programme, Chairman Mr J.W. Gibson wrote that he was grieved that he could not welcome supporters back to a fully developed stadium which he had in mind, but he hoped to do something about the stand before the following season. With a kick-off time of 6.30, large numbers headed for the ground straight from work and such was the congestion around the ground that many of the 41,748 spectators were late in arriving, and missed the kick-off. United celebrated their return with a decisive 3-0 victory in what was a rather untidy ninety minutes with both sides scorning easy opportunities to add to the scoreline.

It was not until the 40th minute that United took the lead, after seeing Downie come close with a shot against the post. A Lynn free kick was contested by Pearson and Gillies, with the latter reaching the ball first only to see it glance off his head and past his own advancing goalkeeper. Mitten added a second from the penalty spot after Rowley had been obstructed in the box by Gillies and Roberts, with the third coming from a Rowley header following another free kick.

The match, however, was not without incident. Midway through the second-half, the referee awarded a free kick against United and as Bolton prepared to take the kick a spectator walked onto the field of play in the direction of the referee, standing near the centre circle. Players and officials stood still, thinking that perhaps he had a message for the referee (other than what was actually on his mind), but before he reached the middle of the pitch the two trainers and a policeman caught up with him and escorted him from the ground.

Spectators could now arrive at the ground by car, bus or train, with the station beside the ground now open for Saturday fixtures. There was no need now to leave your bicycle behind the ground for four pence as in the 1930's, and also gone was the sight of a young lad carrying a blackboard round the ground with the team changes on it, as a new public address system had now been installed. This also enabled the 70 or so volunteer ground stewards to move the crowd into less full areas of the terracing as the stadium filled up.

Cover and seating in the old stand were available for the first visit to Old Trafford by a foreign club side on May 12th 1951, when Red Star Belgrade from Yugoslavia played a friendly as part of the Festival of Britain. Although the scoreline records a 1-1 draw, the visitors were by far the better team, playing some superb football to whet the appetite of the 41,000 crowd.

Always a yard faster and more precise with their passing, they scored after only three minutes through centre forward Zicanovick, with their first shot at goal. Surprisingly, they failed to capitalise further on their productive play. United somehow withstood the seemingly non-stop pressure, thanks mainly to Chilton and Redman, and salvaged a draw eight minutes from time with a Rowley penalty after Aston was brought down inside the area.

Improvements were being made on and off the pitch, with the playing side having won the F.A. Cup in 1948, reaching the semi finals again the following year, as well as finishing runners-up in the League on three occasions. Ground developments continued, with a laundry being built underneath the terracing at the Warwick Road end, with a half time scoreboard appearing at the same end during the summer of 1950.

September 26th 1951 saw the first visit of a non-European team to Old Trafford, Hapoel of Tel Aviv. The strange kick-off time of 5.25 attracted only a 12,000 crowd, but those present were treated to a fine afternoon's football with United winning 6-0. The visitors began the match playing some attractive football, but they did not have the physical presence to break down the United defence. As the game progressed, United began to take command and in a 35 minute spell scored six without reply. The goals coming from Rowley(2), Pearson(2), Aston and Walton.

Scoring six in a friendly was all very well, but it was performances at League level that really mattered and as season 1951-52 began to unfold, it became clear that whatever improvements were made to the stadium, they would pass almost unnoticed to the supporters, as on the field of play the team at last began to look like winning the Championship. On Monday April 21st, Chelsea visited Old Trafford, and a 3-0 victory put United within touching distance of the trophy, thanks to goals from Pearson, Carey and a McKnight own goal. Five days later, however, Arsenal journeyed north to Manchester needing to win 7-0 to steal the championship from United's grasp. Old Trafford had certainly witnessed seven goals at the end of ninety minutes, but the Londoners had only scored one of these in reply to United's six, with Jack Rowley the thorn in the visitors side with a notable hat-trick.

With only eight minutes gone, any fear of being overtaken on goal average disappeared when Rowley scored following a defensive error. Eleven minutes later the Arsenal defence suffered a second

early blow when centre-half Shaw had to leave the field with an injury. United showed little clemency and kept the Gunners under constant pressure, with Rowley again coming close. His drive hit the bar, bounced on the goal line and was frantically cleared amid cries of 'goal' from the United players. As the minutes ticked away towards the interval, United went further ahead with two goals in sixty seconds. Pearson's goal-bound shot went in with a deflection to make it 2-0, while Byrne made it 3-0 with what could be considered the best goal seen at Old Trafford all season. Rowley robbed Forbes and tricked Mercer before passing the ball into Byrne's path. A Carey lob forward to Rowley was hooked over Swindon's head for No.4, while the man of the match gratefully accepted a penalty for his hat trick and United's fifth.

Arsenal were now well and truly defeated and United hit yet another nail into their coffin with Pearson scoring in full stride from a Rowley through ball. The luckless Londoners did score in between all the United action, but it was a mere consolation effort and did nothing to upset the rhythm of the Champions.

As the final whistle blew, many of the 53,651 crowd clambered over the fencing surrounding the pitch to congratulate their favourites. The Beswick Prize Band played 'See the Conquering Hero Comes' as the ecstatic supporters gathered in front of the main stand around the mouth of the tunnel chanting *"We Want Carey"*.

So, Champions at last and the hope that more honours would follow. The first opportunity to add to the trophy cabinet came as early as the following September, when as League Champions they faced F.A. Cup Winners Newcastle United in the F.A. Charity Shield at Old Trafford on the 24th of the month. A big occasion, and one that the BBC felt worthy of a larger audience, for they decided to show live television from Old Trafford for the first time.

'Television At the F.A. Charity Shield Match on Wednesday Evening', proclaimed the front page of the Radio Times for that particular week, and on page 47 was an action picture of the previous Old Trafford meeting between the two sides with shots of both captains - Carey and Harvey - underneath.

Unfortunately television in those days was not what it is today and coverage did not begin until 6pm, and finished at 6.50, therefore providing the viewers with only the second half. Fortunately for those who owned a television, the second forty-five minutes were the most exciting, with five of the six goals scored coming in this period.

United began the match in a flourish with Byrne hitting the post after only two minutes, but Newcastle soon settled and opened the scoring through Keeble. Play proceeded to drift from end to end, and shortly before the interval Byrne again came close to scoring when his shot was cleared off the line by Stokoe. With the television sets switched on, United began to entertain. Three minutes after the break they drew level through Rowley, following fine work by Byrne and Downie.

Four minutes later the homesters were in the lead, with Byrne yet again in the heart of the action. Interchanging passes with Gibson, they set up Rowley for his second. Play began to settle after the frantic start to the second-half, but it was certainly providing absorbing viewing for those in front of the televisions, as well as giving those gathered on the Old Trafford terracing their money's-worth. The lead was increased in the 63rd minute, as Newcastle began to have difficulty in containing United. Rowley found Downie, whose pass inside was collected by Byrne, who shot past Simpson and earned some reward for his earlier play. Newcastle, to their credit continued to try and penetrate the United defence, and were rewarded with a second goal from Keeble after 68 minutes.

This seemed to give United a gentle nudge as they proceeded to step up the play again and Rowley, a constant threat to any defence, provided Downie with goal number four. Unfortunately, Rowley was kicked as he headed the ball through to Downie and had to leave the field. But even against only ten men, Newcastle could not pull back any further goals.

The rebuilding work in and around the stadium had finally brought it back to normality, much to the relief of directors and spectators alike. In Matt Busby's eyes, however, there were other plans and rebuilding work that would soon have to be implemented. This did not concern bricks and cement but footballers. The players who had borne the brunt of resurrecting the club after the war, bringing it back into the spotlight, were now approaching the twilight of their careers and waiting on the sidelines were some highly promising youngsters who were already making a name for themselves in the United Youth team. Slowly the line ups changed as Delaney, Carey, Pearson, Cockburn etc. no longer appeared, while in their place came the likes of Pegg, Edwards, Whelan, Violett, Berry and Taylor. As the 1950's began to unfold, it soon became clear that an exciting period in the club's history was beginning to unfold.

Football today can be a costly form of recreation, but what did the United supporter of the mid-fifties have to pay out to watch his favourites? Admission to the ground was 2/-(10p), juniors 9d(4p), covered terrace 3/6d(17½p), juniors 2/-(10p). Unreserved seats in A and E blocks were 5/-(25p), while reserved seats in B and C were 6/6d(32½p). For those parting with their hard earned cash at the turnstiles on the opening day of season 1955-56, grandstand patrons had the added bonus of some 3000 extra seats after some reconstruction work, which also provided new refreshment bars below stands A and E.

Around the ground other work had been carried out in the summer break, which included up-to-date offices, reconditioned dressing rooms, and recreational facilities for the players. The latter came in for high praise when used for the first time on the opening day of the season for the match against Tottenham.

The second home fixture, against West Bromwich Albion three days later on August 27th, saw Old Trafford used as something of a guinea pig by the BBC. They filmed the match, and then rushed it to Ringway Airport for a flight to London, where it was then taken to their studios to be put through the processing labs. However, it wasn't seen on any television screens as it was a dummy run for a new Saturday night sports programme entitled 'Sports Special' which was to begin on September 10th.

The training ground at the Cliff had enjoyed the luxury of floodlights for some six years, but United had only given brief consideration to installing them at Old Trafford. Writing in the Manchester Evening Chronicle on November 5th 1955, Matt Busby revealed that the installation of floodlights had been delayed due to more important work having to be carried out, but once the necessary work was completed then the directors would look closely at the need for floodlighting. The type they wanted to install was very expensive but would be the best in the country.

The Manchester 'derby', on the last day of 1955 produced some amazing scenes outside and inside the ground. An hour before the kick-off, there were some 35,000 inside, and by the time the teams ran out onto the pitch this had increased to 60,956, creating a post war-record. The turnstiles, however, had closed ten minutes before kick-off, with thousands still outside the stadium. There was chaos everywhere, even though the turnstiles had been in full operation with the queues forming and re-forming rapidly with masses of people shoulder to shoulder trying to obtain entry. The scene looking towards the Warwick Road railway bridge was just as dramatic with the crowd so thick that it was almost impossible to get across.

Extra police had to be called out as the streets around the ground were like a sea of human heads, with the traffic virtually at a halt. Coaches trapped in the traffic jam nearer the ground dropped off their passengers and turned back from where they had come. Thousands of fans unable to gain entry hung around Warwick Road in the hope of the gates re-opening, which they actually did, but only to let people out who could not see or who found the crush inside all too much. These unfortunates outside could not even catch any of the empty buses home, as the drivers and conductors were inside at the match!

As for the match itself, goals from Tommy Taylor and Dennis Violett gave United a 2-1 victory to end the year on a satisfactory note. As 1956 unfolded, United clearly had their sights on the League Championship and with three games still to play they led the table with 55 points from their 39 games with nearest rivals Blackpool on 49 points from only 38 games. The title crunch was to come

at Old Trafford on Saturday April 7th when the Seasiders visited Manchester.

As expected, the gates were locked some fifteen minutes before kick-off, with an enthusiastic 10,000 still outside and a new post war record attendance 62,277 inside. On finding the gates being locked, the thousands outside began frantic attempts to gain entry. Squads of police, some mounted, struggled to bring order to the melee of rushing supporters.

Inside, Blackpool's live duck mascot, accompanied by his 'eastern prince' who took the field along with the team, certainly brought them some early luck as the visitors took a two minute lead through Durie from a Mudie lob. United were soon out for the equaliser with both Violett and Doherty coming close, the latter heading against the post. Play was mainly concentrated around the visitors goal, as the first half progressed. Berry was beginning to have the better of the Blackpool defence and at one point beat five men, crossed to Doherty whose shot beat Farm in the Blackpool goal, only to see Firth clear off the line. Blackpool held on for all they were worth, as the fervent Manchester support urged on the red shirts, but the score remained the same as the half-time whistle blew.

The second half resumed where the first left off and Pegg should have levelled the scoring in almost the first attack. Both sides were then reduced to ten men following a clash of heads between Taylor and Wright, and it was during this period that United finally drew level. Berry, again tantalizing the Blackpool defence found Doherty, who was quickly brought down following a challenge by Farm. Penalty!

Byrne the regular penalty-taker made no move to take this particular kick, so the thorn in the Blackpool side - Berry - strode up and despatched the ball firmly past Farm. As the crowd went ecstatic, both teams returned to full strength and the remaining 35 minutes were going to be a test of nerves, both on and off the pitch. Play drifted around the pitch as the minutes ticked away, and with only ten remaining, it was that man Berry, again, taking on the now exasperated Blackpool defence. His cross was close to 'keeper Farm, but the ball eluded his clutches and fell to Taylor, a yard from the goal line, who managed to put the ball in with his knee, as a defender dived to try and prevent the goal. United were Champions.

Two weeks later, on April 21st, Old Trafford had something of a carnival atmosphere, as Portsmouth brought the curtain down on a triumphant season. United ran out to a tumultuous reception and gave their support a pleasant surprise when they walked to the centre circle and bowed to each section of the ground in turn, as a tribute to the support they had received throughout the season. Unfortunately, the match itself did not live up to the occasion, and a solitary Viollet goal in the 18th minute, was all the 38,400 crowd saw. Shortly before the end, the referee's whistle for a free kick was taken as full-time by sections of the crowd who ran onto the pitch. Play was held up until police cleared the over jubilant fans from the pitch, but minutes later there was an even bigger invasion as the final whistle did blow and supporters surged forward for a better view of the Championship trophy being presented by Mr. Joe Richards of the League Management Committee to Roger Byrne.

Winning the Championship brought an invitation to compete in the European Cup, a competition inaugurated the previous season by the French sports paper 'Le Equipe' and involving the Champions of various European countries. The Football League had thwarted the hopes of the 1955 League Champions, Chelsea, in the first competition, but United were determined to bring European football to Manchester and at the same time gain a wider knowledge of the game outside English shores.

With all European ties being played mid-week, the United directors had to approach neighbours City once again for the loan of their Main Road ground, as they were one step ahead of United with floodlights already having been installed. United revealed their own plans for floodlights at Old Trafford in the United Review for the match against Portsmouth on September 1st. Illustrated on the front was a model of the stadium complete with pylons, and the accompanying text stated that each pylon would be 160 feet high with 54 lights on each one - equal to millions of candle power - and the whole installation would be controlled by a single press button. It was expected that the work would be completed early in 1957 at a cost of over £40,000.

As season 1956-57 unfolded, United were challenging on three fronts - the League, F.A. Cup and European Cup. In Europe, Anderlecht, Borussia Dortmund and Athletico Bilbao had all been brushed aside under the Main Road lights with some of the best football Manchester had ever seen. By April, United were in the semi-finals of the European Cup, had reached the Final of the F.A. Cup and were only a couple of points away from retaining their League title.

F·L·O·O·D·L·I·G·H·T·S at OLD TRAFFORD

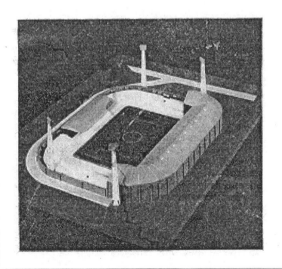

According to electrical experts we should soon have a flood-lighting system as good, if not better, than any other installation in the country! From the model photographed here you will see four pylons each to be 160 feet high. At the top of each tower will be 54 flood-lights - equal to millions of candlepower - and the whole installation will be controlled by a single push-button. The work has been commissioned and completion is expected early in the new year.

The erecting of the floodlights had gone according to plan and were to be used for the first time when near neighbours Bolton Wanderers visited on March 23rd. This gave Bolton the joint distinction of being the first visitors after the war and also the first under floodlights. The sky around Old Trafford was bright in the evening air with the illuminated glow from the new floodlights, (three of which were situated outside the ground), as the supporters made their way towards the ground. They seemed to be attracted like moths as they hurried on their way.

Unfortunately, not all managed to gain entry as the gates were closed about half an hour before the kick off. It was later reported that some 15,000 were stranded outside with 60,862 shoulder to shoulder inside. Not only were the lights a first for United, but they surprised their supporters by taking the field in an all red strip, and while the press hand-out said that the lights would produce the effect of continuous sunlight, the ninety minutes which followed produced nothing but gloom to the United contingent.

Twice in the opening stages, Gubbins came close as United struggled to put their game together, and after thirty minutes the visitors eventually took the lead. A crossfield pass from Lofthouse found Gubbins, whose forward pass to Parry was blasted past Ray Wood. David Pegg came close to an equaliser, as did emergency centre-forward Duncan Edwards and Johnny Berry, but it was the visitors who continued to impress.

Within four minutes of the game resuming after the interval it was 2-0 to Bolton, with a controversial goal. McGuinness was fouled, and with the linesman flagging for the free kick Bolton counter attacked. Full back Hartle, still some distance from goal decided to try his luck with a shot, and was as surprised as anyone to see his effort fly past Wood, via the head of Foulkes. Booing echoed around the ground, but the referee was unmoved and the goal stood. United proceeded to storm the Bolton goal, but to no avail as the Burnden Park side held out until the final whistle.

So, Maine Road did not have to be borrowed for the semi-final European Cup-tie against the reigning champions and world famous Real Madrid. Television rights for the match were secured by Granada and it was to be broadcast live, much to the disappointment of the BBC who were caught by surprise with their rivals move. Granada, however, were faced with a few problems during the build-up to the game. Planning to use three cameras, finding ideal positions for them proved difficult. Each side of the ground had covered accommodation and placing cameras near the half way line would mean blocking the view of some spectators. Using the ends behind the goals, they would be above the heads of the crowd but perhaps too far from some of the action. A camera in the main stand would mean the removal of some seats and as architects, along with stress and strain experts were called in, it was even suggested that part of the stand roof could be cut away to accommodate the camera. In the end ideal positions were found behind the goals and along the side and everyone was happy, except the BBC.

Colourful scenes for the Real Madrid match. Note the TV gantry (top right)

Outside Old Trafford on the night of the match, the Manchester Evening Chronicle gave out thousands of red and white caps and red and white megaphones in the hope of making it the most colourful and noisiest night in the United's history. Leading up to the kick-off, the police gave away hundreds of tickets outside the ground as supporters with spares found it difficult to get rid of them and not wanting to miss any of the match handed them to the police.

Even the touts had difficulty selling their wares, offering £1 tickets for 4/- (20p). The match itself was always going to be a big test for United against the experienced Spanish champions, as they were already 3-1 down from the first leg in Madrid.

Five free kicks in the opening five minutes, four against Madrid, set the pattern for the remainder of the evening. The Spaniards advantage was increased after 25 minutes through Kopa and 7 minutes later Rial, who had provided Kopa's goal, made it 2-0. After the interval, however, United began to put their game together, but it proved too late. Tommy Taylor fired a 61st minute shot in off the post and Bobby Charlton managed a consolation goal four minutes from time. Although there were numerous claims that the referee had blown his whistle at least five minutes early, United were outplayed and out thought by the Spaniards, but their day would surely come.

The League Championship was retained, but dreams of a double celebration collapsed at Wembley, mainly due to goalkeeper Ray Woods injury, as Aston Villa recorded a 2-1 victory.

One unusual incident did occur on December 22nd, when United were scheduled to play West Bromwich Albion. Ready at Old Trafford were a crowd, the United team, a referee and linesmen, but no West Brom., or Matt Busby for that matter. Matt had travelled to Brussels to watch forthcoming European Cup opponents Bilbao play Honved, but the train in which he was returning to Manchester in from London was held up in the Midlands due to fog. He 'phoned his son Sandy and asked him to come to Crewe and pick him up to enable him to make the game. Meanwhile, at Old Trafford, the kick-off was delayed from 2.15 to 2.30, but still no West Brom. It was 4.00pm before they eventually arrived in Manchester, but by that time the game had long since been postponed and everyone had gone home!

Early in September 1957, United held their AGM announcing profits of £39,784 and also their intention of raising the capacity of the ground to 100,000. Some supporters had recently voiced their opinion that the club should consider covering the popular side of the ground, so they were more than happy with the news.

The plans, according to the directors, were well in hand, and would see a new double-decker stand erected as well as the much requested cover on the popular side. Work was scheduled to begin the following year.

On the field, the team were going from strength to strength. Their style of football was admired throughout the country and the players were now all household names; it was to be only a matter of time before the line- up consisted of eleven full internationals.

The season was progressing as the previous one had, and again expectations were high for both domestic and European success. Wolves looked to be the only opposition in the League, Sheffield Wednesday were the next F.A. Cup opponents ,and a trip to Belgrade to defend a 2-1 first leg lead was all that stood between another European semi-final place.

Against Red Star in Belgrade, a creditable 3-3 draw was achieved, and while the players prepared for their journey home, Old Trafford was a hive of activity. The ground staff were busy preparing the stadium for the Saturday League fixture against title challengers Wolves. Office staff, on the other hand were just as busy, making final preparations for not only the Wolves match, but also had the additional burden of dealing with ticket applications for the forthcoming F.A. Cup tie against Sheffield Wednesday.

Shortly after 3pm, however, all the hustle and bustle ceased as a telephone call brought the news that the plane carrying the players and staff had crashed attempting to take off from Munich airport following a re-fuelling stop. With no further details available everyones thoughts went into overdrive, all hoping that the accident would be exaggerated and would not turn out to be too serious.

Soon the news of fatalities came through, but with no names. The telephone lines were now red hot, with the 'phones ringing non-stop, and people were now beginning to gather outside the ground on the stadium forecourt, as the media began to break the news to Manchester and the rest of the country.

Evening Chronicle

No. 78,858   MONDAY, FEBRUARY 10, 1958   A KEMSLEY NEWSPAPER   2d

Berry and Edwards still in danger: Busby improving

UNITED VICTIMS WILL LIE AT OLD TRAFFORD TONIGHT

LATEST BULLETIN

BERRY—
Still in acute danger

BUSBY—
Considerably Improved

EDWARDS—
Still in acute danger

FRANK TAYLOR—
Considerably improved

BLANCHFLOWER—
Considerably improved

MRS. MIKLOS—
out of acute danger but still seriously ill

WOOD, CHARLTON, VIOLLET & TOMASEVIC MORGANS.—all good

SCANLON—
Unsatisfactory but not dangerous

CAPTAIN RAYMENT—
Still in acute danger

Funerals to be private

THE bodies of ten of the dead in the Manchester United disaster will

Trafford was swarming with people desperate for any snippets of news from Germany, as the Championship flag flew at half mast from the stand roof. Earlier preparations for the games against Wolves and Sheffield Wednesday had been in vain, as both were postponed, with the Sheffield cup-tie rearranged for February 19th.

Those who had been queuing for cup-tie tickets were among the first to hear the news, but for some the opportunity to purchase a ticket never came, as sales were immediately suspended and the ticket office closed. Entry into the main office was barred to all except club personnel, and eager journalists, quickly despatched to the ground, had to join the growing crowd outside.

Inside, assistant manager Jimmy Murphy sat devastated beside the telephone, having arrived minutes after the news came through, and to be told by secretary Alma George. Also there were Les Olive, Joe Armstrong and Fred Owen. Police were called to try and disperse the crowds outside, but few were keen to move. The crowd was soon enlarged by workers from the nearby factories as the five o'clock hooters blew and they rushed through the gates quicker than normal to hear more about the rumours that had swept through their buildings earlier. Only hours earlier the talk had been of the creditable draw in Belgrade and the chances of beating Wolves on Saturday, now it was past memories.

The following day saw Manchester in mourning, and like the previous afternoon and evening, Old

The night of February 10th saw the tears and memories flow back, with the bodies of the `Babes' coming home. At 9.35 the BEA Viscount landed at Ringway Airport, 70 minutes late, and one by one the brown coffins and 58 wreaths were carried from the plane to the waiting seventeen hearses, as the League Championship flag flew at half mast above the terminal building.

At 11.15 the coffins were ready to begin the solemn journey to their various destinations. Those of Roger Byrne, Eddie Colman, Geoff Bent, Mark Jones and Tommy Taylor, along with Bert Whalley, Walter Crickmere and Tom Curry, Alf Clarke and Tom Jackson were taken to Old Trafford to lie in the gymnasium, while the bodies of the other journalists and local businessman Willie Satinoff, were taken to private addresses. The coffins of Liam Whelan and David Pegg had been off-loaded during a stop at London.

Despite the late hour, and ignoring the rain that had begun to fall, thousands lined the ten mile route to

Old Trafford, with many kneeling in prayer as the cortege passed by. The largest crowd in the club's history had turned out to pay their respects to the dead Red Devils who had come back home. By the time Old Trafford was reached, the crowds had thickened and it was difficult to tell if it was tears or rain that dampened the faces of both the young and old who huddled together. Slowly the crowd dispersed as the now empty hearses turned away from the ground, and by 2.00am all was silent around the shadowed stadium, with a dim light sneaking out from under the gymnasium door where the bodies lay at rest.

As a new dawn broke over Manchester and the first streaks of daylight filtered through the gymnasium windows overlooking the railway line, the coffins lay on black cloth topped tables with numerous wreaths and flowers placed along the wall-bars, while outside supporters began to reappear on the forecourt. Players and officials arrived at the ground later that dismal morning to gather in the gym, where for several silent moments they stood with heads bowed and with thoughts elsewhere. As the morning passed, relatives of those who lay in the gym arrived to take the coffins to various destinations for their final journey, with the coffin of the youngster from just up the road, Eddie Colman, the first to leave.

Life had to go on, but around Old Trafford everything seemed to be moving at half pace, however, the Sheffield Wednesday F.A. Cup-tie was drawing closer. It was one of those games that everyone, not only United supporters, wanted to attend, and on the night of February 15th, people began to assemble outside the ground beside the ticket office to make sure they were there when the office opened at 10 o'clock the following morning. In the morning, those who had braved the cold night were soon joined by many others, and in what seemed to be no time at all, there was a six deep crowd around the ground. This prompted the ticket office to open for business an hour earlier.

Limited to one ticket per person, the 18,000, 2/- (10p), tickets were sold within four hours. Some, however, had managed to evade the scrutiny of the mounted and foot police, making second visits to the ticket windows to obtain additional tickets which were later sold at more than double the face value. Even on the night of the match, the occasion did not deter the unscrupulous ticket touts who were now asking £1 for 6/6d (32½p) tickets in the city centre. Outside the ground as the minutes to kick off ticked away, it was 30/- (£1.50p) for a 2/- (10p) ticket and £5 for a 7/6d (37½p) seat in the stand.

Old Trafford was a hive of activity with supporters arriving early to savour the dramatic occasion. Black ties, armbands, red, and black rosettes, red and white scarves with a black cross sewn beside the names of the players that had been laboriously embroidered on them months before, seemed to be the dress of the day as the stadium forecourt filled with people. Three hours before kick-off the ground was packed. The players tunnel was bathed with the lights of the newsreel and television cameras, alongside press photographers jostling for the best camera angles, as Bill Foulkes led the red-shirted United team onto the pitch.

The tumultuous roar of the crowd reached an unbelievable level and acted as a signal for those outside with tickets that they had not much time left to get inside, and for those without that the long awaited match was near to starting and they would not be able to relate to their children and grandchildren that 'they were there'.

Around 30 cameramen invaded the pitch for photographs following the one minute silence, as captains Bill Foulkes and Albert Quixall tossed for ends, and then quickly scurried off to vantage points behind the goals so as not to miss any of the action. They had to be quick, as the game began at a frantic pace with the unfamiliar United team showing no signs of nerves or inexperience, giving Wednesday little chance of settling.

With just over 25 minutes gone, United won a corner which was taken by the young untried 19 year-old Shay Brennan. His kick swirled in the evening breeze and somehow drifted past the outstretched arms of Sheffield Wednesday's goalkeeper Ryalls, and dropping into the net to give United the lead. At 7.58, the rebirth of Manchester United had begun. The noise from the 59,848 crowd matched that at the start of the game and seemed to give United an extra man as Wednesday crumpled under the sheer passion of the occasion and the fervent play of the red-shirted unfamiliar eleven.

The visitors managed to subdue the red tide for the remainder of the first half and the opening stages after the interval, but with twenty minutes to go they went further behind. A Pearson shot was only blocked by Ryalls, following some good work by Dawson, and Brennan was there to claim his second goal of the night. If Wednesday felt beaten at the start then they knew they were now and could only wish for the final whistle to arrive. However, a third goal was still to come, six minutes from the end, when Pearson set up Alex Dawson to score with a fine drive. The result not only gave United a passage into the next round of the F.A. Cup, but it brought some life back into the club, giving everyone a lift. Maybe United could go on.

The tears of joy, however, soon turned to tears of sadness as two days later Duncan Edwards died. The colossus from Dudley had suffered multiple injuries in the crash and had struggled to survive in the Munich hospital, but after fifteen days, defeat finally came.

The following day Nottingham Forest visited Old Trafford and the match was preceded by a memorial service. Four hours before kick-off there were queues at the turnstiles and by one o'clock, with an estimated 20,000 outside, the gates were closed. The interdenominational service was conducted by the Dean of Manchester, the very Reverend Herbert A. Jones, and was attended by the Lord Mayor of Manchester Alderman Leslie Lever MP and the Mayor of Salford and Stretford. Originally a tribute to those who had died, it had now become more poignant by the death of Duncan Edwards. Relatives of some of the deceased players were amongst the silent crowd, but for one, Molly Leach, Duncan's fiancée, it proved too much and she left the ground in tears.

During the short prayers, the ground was silent, with snowflakes flickering through the afternoon air. Both teams remained in their dressing rooms during the emotion-charged service and were welcomed onto the pitch with a tremendous reception when the service ended.

Forest, like Sheffield Wednesday before them, were on a hiding to nothing and the young United side once again found themselves elevated to a level superior to their experience. The post-war record crowd of 66,123 were stunned to a second spell of silence in the 30th minute, when Forest took the lead through Imlach, proving that they were not there simply to make up the numbers. United had by then missed several good scoring chances and continued to do so as the match progressed. Although most of the play was in the Forest half United could not turn their play into goals, until 15 minutes from the end, when Dawson scored from a Pearson corner. The United show continued to roll.

An away cup tie at West Brom. followed and yet again United defied the odds, earning a creditable 2-2 draw in a game described at the time by Daily Express reporter Desmond Hackett as *"The greatest game I have ever seen"*. The replay produced another dramatic night at Old Trafford, earning the headlines on both the front and back pages of the national newspapers. *"90,000 in Cup Storm"* proclaimed the Express, while *"Chaos For A Mile Around Manchester United Ground"* appeared on the front of the News Chronicle and Daily Despatch.

The gates were locked at 6.30 and people heading from the ground met those still making their way to the ground. At Central Station 6,000 were waiting in two queues and shouting angrily when it was announced over the loudspeakers that the gates at Old Trafford had been closed and British Rail were running no more trains to the ground. The Daily Express staff reporter wrote *"a near riot flared before the game"*, as fans who had rushed from work found that they had no chance of seeing the match, with around 60,000 in and 30,000 outside the ground. Three mounted policemen managed to subdue the potential trouble, but two men were still arrested, as ticket touts offered 7/6d (37½p) reserved seats for £7 and sold them easily. Police loudspeaker vans warned the traffic packing the roads within a two mile radius of the ground that it was full, but to no avail.

Some youths tried to gain entry to the 2/- (10p) section by climbing up ten foot high glass topped walls, but two policemen caught one of them and led him away, under a hail of bottles, cans and half eaten oranges as the unruly crowd pressed forward. As a police sergeant on horseback tried to aid the constables he was almost pulled from his mount, while another youth was brought down from one of the floodlight pylons by an officer who had to climb 75 feet to reach him.

Fifteen minutes before the kick off the ringleaders of the mob began to batter the turnstile doors, with two being torn off their hinges. Police managed to prevent anyone gaining entry, as others prevented similar occurrences at different gates around the ground. Chief Superintendent Frederick Waddington, head of the Manchester Division of the Lancashire County Police said afterwards - *"In 22 years of controlling crowds at Old Trafford, I have never seen anything like it"*. As for the match, the unbeaten run continued as a solitary Colin Webster goal was enough to take United into the F.A. Cup semi-finals.

Every match at Old Trafford seemed to conjure up an occasion to remember, and West Bromwich Albion's second visit in a matter of days, this time on League business saw the packed ground roar its appreciation to the doctors and nurses of the Rechts der Isar hospital in Munich, and minutes later fall silent as the words of manager Matt Busby echoed around the ground in a recorded message from his hospital bedside.

"Ladies and gentlemen" , it began, *"I am speaking from my bed in the Isar Hospital, Munich, where I have been since the tragic accident of just over a month ago.*

You will be glad, I am sure, that the remaining players here, and myself, are now considered out of danger, and this can be attributed to the wonderful treatment and attention given to us by Professor Maurer and his wonderful staff, who are with you today as guests of the club.

I am obliged to the Empire News for giving me this opportunity to speak to you, for it is only in these last two or three days that I have been able to be told anything about football, and I am delighted to hear of the success and united effort made by all at Old Trafford.

Again it is wonderful to hear that the club have reached the semi-final of the F.A. Cup, and I extend my best wishes to everyone.

Finally, may I just say God bless you all".

Tears were unashamedly shed as the soft Scottish brogue drifted around the ground, but as the message came to an end, loud vibrant cheering took over. The appreciative noise continued as the Lord Mayor of Manchester and the Mayor of Stretford led Professor Maurer, his wife, members of his staff and the deputy Mayor of Munich onto the Old Trafford turf to be shown the gratitude of the United supporters. A section of the crowd began to sing *"For He's A Jolly Good Fellow"* to the Professor, while Bill Foulkes, Harry Gregg and Bobby Charlton presented the nurses with flowers.

Sunshine broke through amid light falls of snow, and once again the gates had opened early as crowds gathered at the ground hours before the kick off.

The third meeting against West Brom. in eight days saw the amazing run of success finally come to an end, as the Midland visitors won 4-0. This defeat did not halt the United youngsters as they overcome Fulham in the F.A. Cup semi-final (after a replay) to reach Wembley on a wave of national emotion.

Lancashire neighbours Bolton Wanderers, however, spoilt a fairy tale ending to the season by snatching the Cup with a controversial goal. The Cup Final normally brought down the curtain on each season, but 1957-58 had been no ordinary one and Old Trafford still had to prepare for one final match. When the season had begun, hopes of success in Europe had been high in everyones mind, after narrowly losing out to Real Madrid the previous term. Now only AC Milan stood between them and the Final, with Old Trafford hosting the first leg on May 8th.

In the opening 45 minutes, it was backs to the wall stuff for the United defence, as Milan began in a determined mood. However, it took the Italians only 24 minutes to gain the advantage. Crowther tried to find Greaves, but his pass was intercepted by Bredesen.

The inside-right quickly found Schiaffino who easily beat Gregg. Some of the United tackling seemed to be a little too enthusiastic, but it was enough to unsettle the visitors, and with only five minutes to the interval, Viollet snapped at a Maldini miss-hit clearance to put the scores level.

If Milan had the better of the first half, United took the initiative after the restart, and goalkeeper Buffon had soon pulled off fine saves from Goodwin and Taylor, while Webster shot over the bar. With only eleven minutes to go and the tie looking like remaining on level terms, an innocuous shoulder charge from Maldini on Viollet, brought a penalty decision from the Danish referee. Inside-right Ernie Taylor placed the ball on the spot, and after much protesting from the Italians, he blasted the ball beyond Buffon, off the underside of the bar.

Old Trafford erupted and the noise threatened to shake its foundations as the crowd kept up their vocal encouragement up until the final whistle. Sadly, it was to prove all in vain, as the return leg in Milan brought little joy. In front of an 80,000 crowd, the one goal advantage was quickly wiped out as Milan cruised to a 4-0 victory, thus ending another bid for European success.

On November 5th 1958, the Old Trafford goal posts were altered to accommodate the Rugby League match between Salford and Leeds. The local Salford club had hired the ground on an experimental basis, to try a match under floodlights. Over 8,000 people turned up, and saw the visiting Yorkshire side win 22-17.

During season 1958-59 more junior turnstiles were opened at the Stretford End in order to admit the growing number of youngsters to attend games with a little more ease. That particular end of the ground came in for more alterations during the summer of 1959, when work began on a new covered stand which would hold over 12,000 supporters.

This would also provide cover for the 22,000 who stood in this section, with admission being 2/- (10p). It was also during this season that all seating was made bookable in advance for first team fixtures.

Numerous suggestion had been put forward for a lasting memorial to those who had lost their lives at Munich. Some had gone as far as to suggest that sections of the ground should be called after individual players, but this was turned down by the board. In the end, a large memorial plaque was decided upon which was to be erected outside the main entrance on the railway side of the ground, while the ground committee were to have a special clock made for a site at the Warwick Road end. A small plaque bearing the names of the journalists who died was to be erected in the Press Box by the Football Writers.

On February 25th 1960, the rain poured down as Manager Matt Busby pulled back the purple drapes which hung over the Munich Memorial Plaque. At the private ceremony were the United players and directors, along with parents, relations and friends of those who died in the disaster. The plaque, designed by a local architect M.J. Vipond, and constructed by Messrs Jaconello Ltd. of Manchester, showed a complete plan of the ground measuring 7'9" by 6'. Green slabs of faience marked out the pitch incised with black and gold glass letters forming an inscription and names of those who lost their lives.

The terraces, gangways and steps were also in faience to scale, and were in a memorial colour of mauve and grey. The stand roofs and perimeter path had been worked from solid quartzite, enclosed by red Barmoral granite forming the boundary wall of the ground. Two teak figures representing a player and spectator stood either side of a laurel wreath and ball, inscribed 1958. The clock, at the Warwick Road end, was inscribed Feb. 6th 1958, Munich, and was unveiled by Mr Dan Marsden the chairman of the ground committee, while the bronze plaque in the press box was unveiled by the only surviving journalist, Mr Frank Taylor.

An interesting inclusion was found in the 'United Review' for the match against Wolves on March 5th. The *"Important Notice"* stated that *"a small boy had suffered a serious eye injury due to another boy firing an air pistol or rifle into the crowd at a previous game."* An early sign of things to come.

Memories of the late 1950's

(Top): Major Ground reconstruction work in 1959.
(Above): The Gymnasium at Old Trafford, with its
sad memories of the aftermath of Munich.
(Left): Floodlight pylon at the scoreboard end.

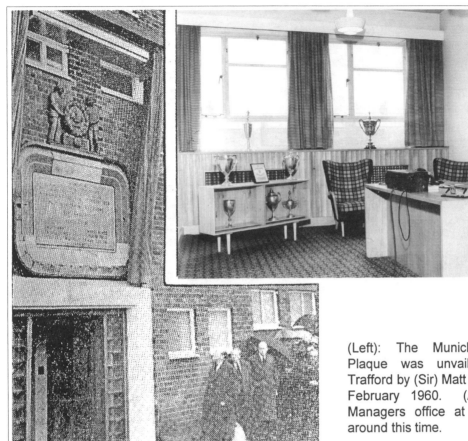

(Left): The Munich Memorial Plaque was unvailed at Old Trafford by (Sir) Matt Busby on 25 February 1960. (Above) The Managers office at the ground around this time.

As the pitch enjoyed a well earned rest during the summer of 1960, further ground improvements were carried out and contractors battled to beat the deadlines set and have the stadium ready for the opening match of 1960-61 against Blackburn Rovers on August 20th. Rebuilding and repairs were carried out at the Stretford End and neighbouring Paddock, and cost between £20,000 and £25,000. This gave the ground a capacity of 66,500, with admission prices for the new section of 3/- (15p) for adults and 1/6d (7½p) for juniors. The following season it was the turn of the United Road section of the ground, which was re-roofed.

The costs of such ventures became increasingly hard to bear, and prompted the setting up of the Manchester United Development Association.

This organisation was formed as a means of raising money to repair and improve the ground in the future. Under the guidance of Bill Burke, it was modelled on a pools scheme which had been set up by Warwickshire County Cricket Club, and from his small office he began bringing in much needed revenue. Their first contribution to ground improvement was installing 1,700 wooden seats at the back of the Stretford End terrace, which became Stand E. These seats were used for the first time on September 25th, when Portuguese club Benfica, the current European Cup holders, visited Manchester for a friendly fixture.

Wednesday October 26th 1960 saw Old Trafford commemorate another milestone in its notable history, when the first Football League cup-tie to be played at the ground took place.

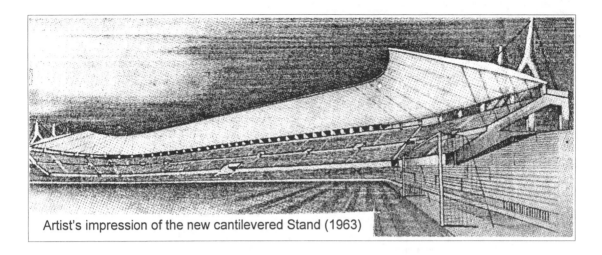

Artist's impression of the new cantilevered Stand (1963)

The visitors, were Exeter City, for a First Round Replay, following a 1-1 draw at St. James Park the previous week. A mere 15,662 turned up at Old Trafford to watch the replay, with United showing their lesser rivals little mercy in a 4-1 win. The goals came from Albert Quixall with two (one a penalty), Johnny Giles and Mark Pearson.

1963 saw the ground development begin on the outside of the stadium, on the section facing the forecourt. The construction consisted of new administration, ticket and development association offices, and it took a local contractor only six months to complete the work at a cost of £14,000.

The sixties were beginning to swing, and popular music was taking on a completely different style as the outlook on life was beginning to change. Crowds at football matches were becoming more vocal in their support, with those at Old Trafford - especially at the Stretford End - no different from others up and down the country. This vocal participation in the game was greatly encouraged by the United management and on Saturday October 26th 1963, pre-match entertainment took on a whole new meaning, with the Ray Bradley troupe of drum majorettes taking on the name of the 'Unitedettes' and introducing the new 'United Song' to the supporters. As the supporters had been singing their own words to the popular tune 'When The Saints Go Marching In', words were composed and printed in the programme for the new song to that particular tune. How many joined in the pre-match community singing is not recorded, but it continued for a few weeks.

1963 also brought the announcement that England were to host the 1966 World Cup and the United directors were honoured by the selection of Old Trafford as one of the stadiums selected as a venue for some of the fixtures in group C. This prompted the board to consider further ground development and it was decided to build a £250,000 cantilever stand along the United Road side of the ground. It would consist of 10,500 seats with covered standing room for a further 10,000 in front. The cantilever roof, measuring 600 feet long by 108 feet wide, would project to the front of the terracing where it would be 48 feet high and be suspended from steel tubes retained by reinforced concrete yolks projecting 30 feet above the rear of the stand.

The building of this new stand was a matter of careful consideration as it left no funds for strengthening the playing squad, which obviously took priority over any structural matters. Manager Matt Busby, however, felt that his squad was strong enough to challenge for the games honours and gave the OK for the money to be spent on the stand.

Running the length of the ground, the stand would turn at the corners and at the south-east link up with the existing standing area. No reduction in capacity would be necessary. Perhaps the most prominent feature would be the installation of 34 private boxes, which could each hold up to six people. They would be taken by businesses to entertain clients and a waiter service would be available, with a private lift to transfer those fortunate to have the use of them from ground level to the heated boxes via a lounge. Centre boxes were to be let at £300 for a season, with those at the side £250. The rental secured admission to all home games and needless to say, all boxes were over-applied for from the start.

An early estimated cost for constructing the new stand was £175,000, but a closer examination took the figure up to £250,000. The final cost, however, was nearer to £320,000, and with only around £75,000 in the bank at this time, it was a major undertaking, putting the club well into the red.

Early in 1965, two separate sections were created at the Stretford End, by erecting a barrier at the United Road side. This prevented spectators from entering the ground on Warwick Road and walking round to the Stretford End, thus causing crowd control problems. On completion of the new stand, a further barrier would be erected at the Old Trafford end, to make these distinct sections, each with its own turnstiles and exits. Capacity would then be 64,000, with 18,500 seated and 52,000 under cover.

Constructing the cantilever stand was not without its problems. Cracking appeared in some of the concrete support columns and tests had to be carried out to correct this. These problems were soon overcome and building work continued to schedule and small sections of the stand became available to supporters towards the end of the season.

On the pitch, a victory over Liverpool left United one point behind Leeds, with two games left, compared to their Yorkshire rivals one. April 26th saw Leeds travel to Birmingham where they only managed a 3-3 draw, while the same day United beat Arsenal 3-1 at home. It was a dramatic night at Old Trafford for everyone connected with the club as they contemplated the outcome of the match at St. Andrews. Best managed to release some of the early tension with a close range effort after only 7 minutes, but a bigger roar was heard at 8.38 when a loudspeaker announcement proclaimed that Birmingham were 3-0 in front, giving spectators and players alike added determination and inspiration, which led to Law making it 2-0 a minute later.

With 23 minutes to go, Crerand fouled Baker in the penalty area, but United 'keeper Pat Dunne brilliantly blocked the spot kick only for Eastham to follow up and net the rebound.

Two minutes past nine, and the loudspeakers crackled into action. Leeds had pulled two goals back. The game was now poised on a knife edge with everyones thoughts wandering to the Midlands, while at the same time trying to concentrate on what was being played out in front of them.

But as the minutes ticked away Law scored a third goal, and the closing stages were played out against a wall of noise. Five minutes later, and it was all over, 3-1 to United and the Arsenal players made for the safety of the dressing rooms as the crowd invaded the pitch. But what of Leeds?

Silence enveloped the crowd on the pitch and on the terracing once again, as the loudspeakers sprung in life. *"The final score from St. Andrews is Birmingham City 3 Leeds (pause) 3".* United were Champions.

On Wednesday May 19th, prior to the Inter Cities Fairs Cup-tie against Strasborg, United were presented with the League Championship trophy. On a perfect spring evening, with the sun shining down on the colourful Old Trafford terraces, the trophy was brought onto the pitch and placed on a small table. The cheering, which had begun at the sight of the trophy, erupted as Denis Law walked alone from the tunnel dressed in a red tracksuit top, to receive the coveted trophy from Mr Joe Richards. Each player then appeared individually to receive his medal and the adoration from the crowd, with George Best bringing up the rear. The biggest cheer, however, was reserved for Matt Busby who followed his team out onto the pitch to receive his medal.

After this presentation, the spotlight drifted back to Denis Law, who had to step forward for a second time, to receive his European Player of the Year award from Max Urbin of France Football. Off the players then went on a lap of honour and the excitement for the night was over as United and Strasborg played out a boring 0-0 draw.

1966: The new Stand and executive boxes, all ready for the forthcoming World Cup matches.

Throughout the summer, work continued around Old Trafford, with the World Cup now less than a year away and becoming much more of a priority to United. By the time season 1965-66 arrived, a large section of the new cantilever stand was ready for occupation, with the final section at the Warwick Road end scheduled to be available in October. Work also had to be carried out below the stand, with alterations to the toilet and refreshment areas adding to the expenditure. Better facilities for the supporters, but what sort of prices did the United fan of the mid-sixties have to pay to sit in what would be known as Stands G and H, or stand in the United Road Paddock, in front of this new construction? To sit in sections G and H, it would cost 10/- (50p) and 12/6 (62½p), bookable two weeks in advance, while the Paddock was 5/- (25p), with no reductions for juniors!

Vocal encouragement was becoming more than just enthusiastic cheering, with many clubs' supporters beginning to compose numerous songs and chants to popular tunes. Liverpool's Kop played a prominent part in this, jumping onto the 'Mersey Sound' bandwagon, but United's Stretford End became just as noted for its vocal participation and soon became the main section of the ground for the standing supporter who was proud to be known as a Stretford-Ender. Unfortunately, some of the crowd participation became a little too boisterous, (no better or worse than that at most other grounds around the country it must be added), and the club were forced on numerous occasions to publish notices asking those responsible to refrain from the throwing of toilet rolls and other objects on to the pitch.

The Inter Cities Fairs Cup-tie at the end of the 1964-65 season against Ferencvaros had witnessed behaviour which had greatly upset the United directors, and manager Matt Busby had been forced to mention it in the club programme. Warning notices were posted around the ground, but those, and the manager's programme notes, were generally ignored. This led to a further warning notice in the programme for the match against Newcastle United on September 15th, referring to the obscene chanting at the referee at the previous home match against Stoke City. During this particular match, eight youths, aged between 15 and 21, had been ejected from the Stretford End and subsequently banned for the remainder of the season.

Building work at the ground caused some congestion in the United Road, and brought the club numerous complaints, forcing them in the end to take some action. Two gates were placed into the barrier which separated the United Road Paddock and the Scoreboard End, giving the spectators additional exits. A further improvement was the erection of a footbridge at the Stretford End of the ground following the granting of permission by the Stretford Council.

When the floodlighting was installed at the ground, the United management must have thought that the problems of evening games had at last been solved. They were, however, soon to find otherwise. The fixture against West Bromwich Albion on December 27th, originally an evening kick off, had to be changed to a 2 o'clock start, as the North Western Electricity Board would not give permission to allow the floodlights to be used, as the match would be played during a 'peak demand' period;

As 1966 unfolded, the final preparations for the World Cup were put into place. The new stand had off- course cost more than £300,000, but the outlay was to increase in order to improve some of the existing facilities for visiting media representatives. The press box, normally capable of accommodating all the journalists who were required to report on United games with ease now had to be enlarged to seat around 400. Some of the seating in the main stand had therefore to be sacrificed, with new seats along with writing tops and telephone points installed. Below the stand, at first floor level, a special press working area was constructed, consisting of every type of communication equipment necessary to cover the three games in group C between Portugal, Hungary and Bulgaria. Old Trafford was ready for the World Cup.

Tickets were available in books of three and were graded into two prices for seating £6-6-0d and £3, while similar arrangements were available for those wishing to stand, with tickets at £1-17-6d and £1-2-6d. To attend one match, standing on the Stretford End would cost 7/6d.(37½p).

Some of the stars from the Portuguese and Hungarian sides had already graced the Old Trafford turf with their club sides, which perhaps had something to do with the rather poor attendances for the three games. The opening match on July 13th, between Hungary and Portugal attracted the best of the three attendances with 29,886, while three days later Bulgaria and Portugal was watched by 25,438. The final match in the group attracted slightly less, with 24,129 passing through the gates. So, the soccer carnival was soon over, with England becoming World Champions. The three years of planning were hailed as a success, with United's involvement receiving many compliments from the visiting media, teams and supporters.

Season 1966-67 soon saw United amongst the pack at the top of the table and in the post World Cup boom, crowds flocked to Old Trafford to enjoy the free flowing, entertaining football produced by messrs. Best, Law, Charlton and company. On October 29th, Arsenal travelled north to Manchester and took part in one of the most bad tempered matches ever seen at the ground. On no less than four occasions, players from both sides faced up to each other as play drifted past. George Best and Peter Storey were the first, in the early stages of the game.

In the 24th minute it was Law and Ure, while six minutes later Crerand and Simpson were at loggerheads, with McLintock and Kidd having a similar involvement not so long after. But it was two tempestuous Scots - Denis Law and Ian Ure, who provided most of the venom in this confrontation. Their initial feud flared up in the middle of the park as early as the 24th minute, when an ugly tackle by the Arsenal defender prompted Law into retaliation, and earning both a booking. Ure continued to keep Law under close scrutiny, with the United man's temper continuing to rise with every tackle and with only seven minutes remaining everything came to a head.

With play at the opposite end of the park, Ure aimed a kick at Law for one reason or another, who in return threw a punch at his international team mate. Numerous players moved in to try and separate the two, and when things had quietened down, both were sent off. Best was lucky not to follow them, after he too threw a couple of punches at an Arsenal player in the melee.

Another memorable game from the early months of this season was against Sunderland on November 26th. This game produced something of a record at Old Trafford, not in the 5-0 scoreline or in activities similar to the previously mentioned encounter, but for the fact that David Herd scored against three different goalkeepers!

Sunderland's regular goalkeeper, Jim Montgomery, was hurt and had to go off eight minutes after Herd opened the scoring. Charlie Hurley replaced him until half-time, but by then United's centre forward had made it 2-0. After the interval, John Parke took over, but fared little better with David Herd netting twice as United scored another three. One of Herd's shots was actually measured at 72mph!

Friday March 3rd saw another first for Old Trafford, even though United were playing away at Highbury against Arsenal. The match was re-arranged, as the League Cup Final between Queens Park Rangers and West Bromwich Albion was being played at Wembley the following day, and it was decided to experiment with closed circuit TV

and beam the pictures back to Manchester, making it the first Division One match to be shown in this way. The match was projected onto seven screens, measuring some 40 feet wide by 30 feet high, situated around the pitch, giving the 28,423 spectators a panoramic view of the match in London.

Opinions on the night's viewing were varied, especially as one of the screens was blown down, but the quality of the camerawork was acceptable, and on the night the crowd soon became involved in the game, which gave the sponsors encouragement for the future.

Familiar scenes were once again in evidence at the final match of the season against Stoke City, when 61,071 spectators saw Sir Joe Richards, President of the Football League, present Denis Law with the League Championship trophy. The match itself was a non-starter with the fans happy to make their own afternoon's entertainment and dispose of their remaining toilet rolls.

With United having won the Championship the previous season, the F.A. Charity Shield brought the curtain up at Old Trafford for 1967-68, with Tottenham Hotspur the visitors. nothing very notable in that, or in the 3-3 scoreline, but the way that one of the Tottenham goals was scored is worth a mention. It will go down as one of the most unusual or bizarre goals ever scored at the ground, with Pat Jennings in the 'Spurs goal the 'scorer. With his back to the Stretford End, he kicked the ball from his hands and watched it soar into the United half, bounce in the United penalty box, and disappear over the head of Alex Stepney into the back of the net. Goal!

Ground development had come to something of a halt following the dramatic transformation for the World Cup. However, in September 1967 a simple construction, out on the Old Trafford forecourt, heralded the beginning of the United Souvenir shop. During the club tour of Australia that summer, the board discussed the possibilities of the club shop and upon returning home it was decided to invest in such a venture, to the sum of £1,000. A small wooden hut was erected, and under the management of Mr Frank Gidley (assisted by his wife, daughter and another female), he began

Friday 3rd March 1967   Number 18   Price sixpence

Souvenir programme
A special edition of the official M.U.F.C. programme to commemorate

THE FIRST FOOTBALL MATCH IN DIVISION ONE TO BE TELEVISED ON CLOSED-CIRCUIT T.V.

ARSENAL v MANCHESTER UTD.
KICK-OFF 7·30 p.m.

DIRECT FROM ARSENAL STADIUM
BY ARRANGEMENT WITH ARSENAL F.C. AND VIEWSPORT LTD.

selling the likes of badges, ties, pennants, photos, bags and key rings to the United supporters.

Over the years, many thousands have visited Old Trafford to enjoy an afternoon, or evening's entertainment, but on December 2nd 1967, the Rt. Hon. Harold Wilson OBE, the Prime Minister, was present at the match against West Brom. The occasion was marked with a full page mention in the programme, as it was the first time that such a celebrity had visited the ground.

Towards the end of the season, on April 29th, the club staged the F.A. Cup Semi-Final between Everton and Leeds United, the first to be held at the ground in post-war years, although it had regularly been the venue prior to the hostilities. A full house of 63,200 was present, producing record receipts for an F.A. Cup Semi-Final of £51,000, with Everton fans turning the Stretford End into a mass of blue and white for the day. It was the visitors from Liverpool who went home singing, following a narrow 1-0 victory. As for United, they had at last achieved their 'holy grail' by winning the European Cup at Wembley, defeating Benfica 4-1 on an emotionally charged May evening.

Interest in the club had always been high, but following the latest triumph things began to escalate, with the recently opened Souvenir Shop becoming an overwhelming success. New premises had to be found to accommodate this runaway business and it eventually moved into the offices of the Development Association, who in turn moved across the forecourt to a completely new home costing £40,000.

To the stadium, there was little in the way of changes, but on the field of play there was much to write about, with the visit of Estudiantes from Argentina producing another 'first', in the way of a World Club Championship Cup-Tie. The first leg, in Buenos Aries, was not without incident and United returned home with only a 1-0 defeat to turn around, but the second leg at Old Trafford was to produce a tempestuous evening as the game unfolded. Hopes of becoming the first British club to win the trophy were high, but these hopes were dashed after only six minutes when the South Americans went 2-0 in front on aggregate. United's chances were further hampered in the 36th minute

when Denis Law was carried off with a gashed knee. United continued to try and create an opening and get back into the game, but with tempers running high after several unsavoury incidents in the 1st leg, which had seen Noddy Stiles being sent off, the match always looked like boiling over.

Numerous opportunities were squandered and as the match moved into the final minutes, with United still trailing, George Best and Medina were ordered off following a fist-throwing melee on the touchline. With the crowd on their toes, Morgan scored in the dying seconds, but it was too late to save the game. Both legs will probably be remembered more for the unsavoury incidents than the football that the World Club Championship brought. An interesting footnote to this game was that the 'United Review' sold a record 74,680 copies on the night, when record ground receipts of £63,438 were taken.

Whilst mentioning programme sales at the ground, the League match against Arsenal on October 15th, saw an incredible 64,772 copies sold. December saw an open letter appear in the club programme relating to recent obscene chanting by large numbers of the spectators in the Stretford End. Whether or not this had any effect on the overall behaviour of these supporters is doubtful, as events later in the season would show.

A re-arranged league match against Queens Park Rangers on March 19th saw another club record set, when the 8-1 scoreline was the highest recorded by the club since changing its name to Manchester United. Many missed the last few goals having left before the end, with the score 4-1, and a mere six minutes to go. Morgan had begun the rout on the half hour, but it was not until the second half that the floodgates were opened.

Best made it 2-0 within five minutes of the restart, with a shot from 12 yards, but Rangers pulled it back to 2-1 after 62 minutes. Three minutes later, however, the two goal advantage was restored when Best scored with a typical effort. A fourth followed from Morgan, after Kidd hit the bar from an Aston corner. That left the four in the final six minutes, when Stiles, Kidd, Aston and Morgan - completing his hat trick - made it a night to remember.

Although struggling in the League, the assault on Europe was more productive with the semi-final stage once again being reached, with AC Milan standing between United and a place in the Final for a second consecutive season. The first leg in Milan on April 23rd was transmitted live to Old Trafford on six giant screens and was a vast improvement on the previous closed circuit showing against Arsenal a couple of years previously. Around 22,500 supporters watched the game on the 40 foot screens, preparing themselves for the real thing in the return leg, 22 days later.

Although the second leg saw United two goals behind, they were confident that they could still obtain a satisfactory result on the night. With the goalless first half presenting little in the way of scoring opportunities for United, all was set for an enthralling second forty-five minute period. However, with only a few minutes of this played, drama unfolded in front of the Stretford End. With play at the opposite end of the ground, a missile was thrown from the crowd, hitting the Milan goalkeeper Cudichni on the back of the head and knocking him to the ground. Play was soon stopped, with the 'keeper flat out in the goalmouth, and as he received attention from the Milan trainer, the hooligan element in the Stretford End cheered and bayed *"we want a riot"*. A loudspeaker announcement was made to warn the crowd that any further throwing of objects would result in the game being abandoned. This was something United did not need as they continued to inflict pressure on the Italians goal.

With 65 minutes gone, a Charlton goal brought revived hope and the ground erupted. The wall of noise gave United inspiration as both the crowd and the players sensed that the goal required to force a play-off would surely come. The closing minutes of the game were played at a frantic pace with Pat Crerand, forever the midfield inspiration of United's attacks, once again setting things in motion. His cross, low from the right, found Law lurking in his familiar position close to goal and his side-footed shot crept slowly towards the Milan net with the 'keeper beaten.

Full back Anquillietti managed to get back and scrambled the ball out of the vacant goalmouth, while Law, with arm raised in salute, was already

claiming the goal as were fellow teammates. The referee, a little behind play, did not share their opinion that the ball had crossed the line, and to everyones amazement waved play on. United's chance was gone. Television pictures would later confirm that the ball had indeed crossed the line, while the repercussions from this match would be felt for some time.

The hooliganism which had sprung to life in the mid-sixties was now common at many grounds around the country, Old Trafford included, and was beginning to cause concern. Due to the missile throwing incident during the Milan match, the board considered erecting fences of some sort behind the Stretford End goal, but prior to the start of season 1969-70 they decided against it, although it was something that they would keep in mind if any similar incidents occurred in the future.

Never a club to sit back and wait for things to happen, with the opening of the souvenir shop a classic example, (a small kiosk was also opened this season in the cantilever stand), United began to plan ahead with further improvements. Chairman Louis Edwards revealed in October 1969 that the board had studied several ideas of constructing a sliding roof over the ground, similar to the Houston Astrodome in Texas, which was fully enclosed and had cost £11 million to build in 1965. This was perhaps rather revolutionary at this time in Britain. Although more immediate plans, such as covering the Scoreboard End, were being considered, the idea of a sliding roof was certainly something for the future.

For the first time since 1911, Old Trafford staged an F.A. Cup Final, when the replay of the 1970 match between Chelsea and Leeds United came north. United had actually lost to Leeds in the semi-final and on the eve of the Final at Wembley had beaten Watford in the first ever third place play-off match. Under the Old Trafford lights, the Londoners defeated United's Yorkshire rivals 2-1 after extra time, in front of 62,000, who paid ground record receipts of £88,000. Over 75,000 programmes were sold for this match creating yet another record.

Earlier in the season, a minor representative match between England and Russia at under 23 level had also been played at the ground, watched by a disappointing crowd of only 19,404.

So, Old Trafford was once again to come under major construction work with another section of the ground being changed beyond recognition and a familiar land mark disappearing.

It was decided that the cantilever stand along the United Road would be extended round behind the Scoreboard End at a

The Scoreboard End in 1970 - soon to change completely.

obtained as exact details of the incident were unclear.

Matt Busby, now general manager, attended the second hearing, along with secretary Les Olive, to speak on behalf of the club. Their thoughts, opinions and pleas were of little avail as the F.A. Committee's verdict was to fine the club a sum of £7,000 and make

cost of £400,000, which would be met by the Development Association. This would create 5,000 new seats with further executive boxes behind, and a paddock for standing supporters in front. Work was to start before the end of the 1970-71 season.

Slight alterations were also made at the Stretford End during 1970-71, but these were forced upon the club and reduced the capacity of the ground by around 1,500. Due to some individuals in that section of the ground failing to take heed of the club's warnings to refrain from throwing objects onto the pitch or at opposing players, an area immediately behind the goal was cleared towards the end of December. This, however, failed to deter such behaviour, as a knife was thrown onto the pitch during the match with Newcastle United on February 27th. The club were called before the F.A. Disciplinary Committee under a charge of crowd misbehaviour, but the first hearing was adjourned so that further evidence could be

them play their first two fixtures scheduled for Old Trafford at the start of season 1971-72 on neutral grounds, not less than 25 miles away. United tried to switch the match against Arsenal to Wembley, but the playing surface was being relaid, ending that hope, and the search for suitable temporary accommodation proved a little difficult at first, as ideal grounds were either too close or their owners were also at home on the dates required.

In the end, Liverpool and Stoke were decided as venues for the 'home' games against Arsenal and West Bromwich Albion, with the match against the Gunners being played on a Friday night. The first fixture at Old Trafford was on September 4th against Ipswich Town.

With work beginning on the extension of the cantilever stand, the familiar half-time scoreboard was soon to disappear from the back of the terracing. No longer would the supporters pass the ten minute break in the action watching the

Work gets underway on the construction of the 'K' Stand (at the Scoreboard End)

numbers appear against the corresponding letters. In its place, came the 63 character addicater - a new electronic scoreboard, placed in the top corner of the cantilever stand J section. This first came into operation towards the end of 1971-72, although many would say that the old manual scoreboard was better, and more reliable, than the new replacement.

New floodlights were also installed under UEFA requirements and of a necessary change due to the colour television coverage. The building work caused some upheaval to supporters who used this end of the ground, as it had done to those on the United Road some years before. New turnstiles were opened on the United Road corner of the ground, with the toilet, exit and catering facilities below standard until progress was made.

The cleared area behind the Stretford End goal remained as it was, even though it was brought up at the AGM when a shareholder complained that it was rather silly turning people away from games when there was accommodation available for some 1,500. It was suggested that wire fencing could be erected as an alternative, but the area remained

vacant. It was re-opened, however, for the start of season 1972-73, and with the cantilever stand at the Scoreboard End now complete, Old Trafford had seating on all four sides and was undoubtedly the best club ground in the country. For a second consecutive season an F.A. Cup semi-final was held at the ground. Liverpool defeated their Merseyside rivals Everton 2-1, while the previous year, Arsenal made a long haul up from London to face, and defeat Stoke City 2-1.

Although the stadium was a superb sight, the playing surface left a lot to be desired. A couple of games had to be postponed due to its muddy state and the failure of the grass growing properly gave groundsman Joe Royle nightmares. Bingley Turf Institute were called in, and following a survey, discovered the newly build stand was preventing a drying wind from circulating around the pitch. This was considered to be only a minor problem, with the real cause producing the poor condition of the playing surface being a layer of compact soil a few inches below ground level.

The job of solving the problem was given to the Cambridge Soil Service, who cut slits in the ground and injected sand into them. This went a long way to improving the condition of the pitch.

Monday April 23rd saw the curtain come down on not only another season, but also marked the last home appearance of one of the great names in the history of Manchester United - Bobby Charlton. Season 1972-73, had been a testing time for all connected with the club, but for the second time in those traumatic days, the man who had begun his United career on the same ground, scoring twice in a 4-2 victory over Charlton Athletic, helped create lingering memories for the supporters.

The first occasion was on September 18th 1972, when 60,538 people turned up to watch United draw 0-0 with Celtic in his testimonial match, and many of those supporters were again present to watch the balding figure emerge from the tunnel to walk between the players of his beloved United and Sheffield United to receive a presentation from the club. Sadly, the visitors had not read the script properly and recorded a 2-1 victory. So ended 20 years at United, and following the final whistle section of the crowd invaded the pitch and began swinging from the crossbars, bringing the day to a sad end.

Building work during season 1973-74 concentrated on the club training ground at the Cliff in Lower Broughton instead of the familiar surroundings of Old Trafford. Government restrictions, due to power strikes saw the club office hours alter and kick off times were brought forward to 2 o'clock as floodlights could not be used.

Since winning the European Cup in 1968 and reaching the semi-finals the following season, team performances had varied from memorable to downright dismal, with the latter being more frequent during this particular season. So much so, that a glance at the League tables saw the name of Manchester United flirting with relegation as the final fixtures of the season were played out. With only two fixtures remaining, it was obvious to all that the result of the penultimate match, against local rivals Manchester City at Old Trafford on April 27th, was going to decide United's fate.

As the sun rose on Manchester that Saturday morning, bringing to life a city divided in its favours, the tension and importance of the match was obvious everywhere. To the City contingent it was an opportunity to send their dearest rivals into the Second Division, giving them more pleasure than any previous victory. Meanwhile, the red and white clad followers winding their way towards Old Trafford hoped that City would perhaps show a little clemency for their struggling neighbours and not give this particular 'derby' match the fire an enthusiasm of past encounters.

Before the kick off, hundreds of youngsters invaded the pitch on several occasions, mainly coming from the Stretford End, keeping the numerous police officers busier than usual, in an attempt to keep the rival factions apart and the pitch clear. As the United players ran out onto the pitch, however, another mini invasion took place.

The game itself was never going to be a spectacle, but in the early exchanges United looked the better side. Corrigan was tested with a cross from Morgan, while Stepney did well to hold one at the opposite end from Summerbee. After 13 minutes, it was United who almost took the lead as Corrigan made a mess of a McIlroy lob, and Donnachie had to head off the line from McCalliog. Another fumble from the big City 'keeper almost let in Daly as United continued to press. With the visitors beginning to exert a little pressure, United were glad to hear the half-time whistle, but the second half resumed where the first had left off and it took United a few minutes to regain their composure, and once again they came close to opening the scoring, with a McIlroy shot being cleared off the line by Barrett.

During the second half the Old Trafford cauldron was boiling over and a fire was lit in the Stretford End behind Corrigan in the City goal. A number of people strayed onto the pitch, causing the referee to take the players over to the touchline until they were removed. It was later revealed that Corrigan had more than a fire behind him to content with, as he had been hit with a dart and a knife had narrowly missed him during the eventful 45 minutes.

As the minutes ticked away eager fans spent more time looking at their watches and listening to other scores on the radio than the match unfolding in

Old Trafford in 1973

front of them. City began to take the upper hand, with Booth heading narrowly over and Oakes shooting wide, both supplied by crosses from the ever dangerous Tueart. With only 7 minutes remaining and a goalless draw beginning to look a likely outcome, City once again moved towards the United goal. A cross from Lee into the crowded goalmouth reached former United hero Law a few yards out, but with his back to goal. Casually he backheeled the ball and to his eternal grief saw it trickle past the wrong footed Stepney into the net. United were down. Law, shunning all congratulations, was immediately substituted, and minutes later all hell was let loose as hundreds invaded the pitch, some attacking City players and the police.

Immediately the referee signalled for the players to leave the pitch, which was now crowded with people, to the hopeful security of the tunnel, as numerous fans were trampled and injured while the police tried to restore order. A line of around 40 police, arms linked, tried to force the invaders back over the perimeter fencing, while over the loudspeakers came the voice of Sir Matt Busby pleading for calm, but to no avail.

With more and more people now finding their way onto the pitch, it became obvious that the game would not re-start, and an announcement to this effect followed soon after, as the police inspector in charge advised the referee that it would be unwise to let the game continue. This led to even more spectators coming onto the pitch and they began to assemble in front of the main stand at the mouth of the tunnel, where a line of 20 policemen prevented anyone from going any further.

Hundreds had been ejected from the ground during the match on a shameful day in the club's history, and it was they - along with those who had on several occasions invaded the pitch - who made the newspaper headlines in the days that followed. Calls were made to close the ground and a record punishment looked to be coming United's way as the afternoon's events began to be digested. Sir Matt Busby said that perhaps cages of some kind would be a solution. The final match of the season, at Stoke a few days later, saw further trouble from United supporters and club officials began a nervous close season wait to see what punishment awaited them.

The Football League later confirmed that the 1-0 scoreline would stand, and in June the United directors decided to take matters into their own hands rather than await the F.A.'s decision, and announced that they would be erecting 9 foot high spiked fences behind each goal at a cost of £4,500. A five man F.A. disciplinary commission visited Old Trafford and were shown two specimen sections of the fencing with safety gates added in case of an emergency. The commission were satisfied with United's move and simply ordered the club to pay their costs, which amounted to less than £200.

Security fencing comes to Old trafford in 1974

So, those attending the opening fixture of 1974-75 at Old Trafford were greeted with the unfamiliar sight of the metal fencing behind either goal. Trouble, however, continued at away games, which United could do little to prevent. One type of supporter that United were happy to accommodate were the blind, and headphones were fitted to six seats in the main stand beside the hospital commentary position for use by such supporters, with the prospect of more to follow.

Before the turn of the year, work begun on rebuilding the main stand which was going to incorporate an executive suite with two restaurants. This plush construction would cost in the region of £500,000 which would soon be recouped in membership fees. The interior decoration, including genuine rosewood panelling, luxurious carpeting and concealed lighting, was reported to be costing around another £70,000.

A large window offered a panoramic view of the stadium, but games would have to be watched from a seat in the stand, which now had a cantilever roof in the centre section, with a separate section reserved for the executive members providing electrically heated seats during winter games. More private boxes were also installed and could be hired at £100, while other minor alterations included an area cleared in front of the Old Trafford Paddock (in front of the main stand) to accommodate wheel chair supporters and the television gantry on the roof of the main stand was enlarged and improved to give cameras a better angle.

Hooliganism, was by now a major problem facing everyone connected with the game and although outbreaks of trouble at Old Trafford was limited to minor scuffles on odd occasions, when the team played away from home it was a different story and many clubs found their ground under seige when the 'Red Army' paid a visit. Every away fixture seemed to cause problems of some sort and an MP called for Old Trafford to be closed for a year following one outbreak of trouble.

A year after the embarrassing scenes that accompanied the match against City, 58,769 packed Old Trafford to salute Martin Buchan and his team as they received the Second Division Championship trophy prior to the final fixture of the season against Blackpool. As the players did a lap of honour, one or two over enthusiastic youngsters managed to get onto the pitch to run alongside the players and the end of match 'annual' pitch invasion was very lighthearted compared to that of twelve months before.

By the beginning of season 1975-76, the Executive Suite Restaurant and Grill Room were catering for members of the public as well as supplying a superb a la carte menu on match days in the former, while the latter catered for those with more simple tastes. The same facilities were also available at lunch times during the week and the weekends and could be hired for banquets, conferences and any other private function. This provided the club with extra revenue, with the limited membership of 300, at a cost of £135, soon being over subscribed.

The building of the Executive Suite had involved extending out from behind the main stand, still enabling team coaches etc. to drive down that side of the ground. It did, however, destroy a familiar landmark at that side of the ground - the Munich Memorial Plaque, above the main entrance. Upon the completion of the new extension, only part of the plaque was still visible. It had been originally planned to remove the plaque and relocate it, but when attempts were made to do so it was discovered to be to firmly attached to the outer wall and could not be removed in one piece. So, the club commissioned a new memorial, identical to the original, which would be sited on the brickwork of K stand at the Scoreboard End of the ground in full view of anyone approaching the ground.

United's final League position for season 1975-76 gained them a place in the UEFA Cup the following term, and with the hooligan element still causing problems it was decided to extend the existing fencing right round the ground to prevent any crowd invasions and stern punishment from UEFA if it occurred during their competition. The 8 foot high fencing would cost £20,000 but it was considered a cheap price to pay to prevent any unnecessary occurrences.

With the prospect of European football returning to the ground, the club installed a new £50,000 floodlighting system. The old lights had deteriorated over the years and the new system was a vast improvement. The reserves were the first to enjoy the benefits in a Central League fixture against Coventry, with the first senior match against Tranmere in the League Cup a few days later.

The Munich clock, the other memorial to those who died in 1958, was also soon to be moved from its original site and also replaced with a new one. It took up a position above the memorial, a few yards around the corner from its original position.

The 1977 F.A. Cup Final victory over Liverpool kept United on the European stage for the second consecutive season and a better performance than that of the previous campaign was hoped for, but as it turned out this was not to be. In the first round, a creditable 1-1 draw in France against St. Etienne was overshadowed by trouble in the stadium prior to kick off, with rival fans involved in vicious exchanges.

UEFA acted quickly and strongly, banning United from the competition, but following an appeal the sentence became a fine of £7,500 and a ruling that the return leg against the French side must be played at least 125 miles from Manchester. Following this announcement, there were no shortages of offers from clubs willing to host the game - from Sunderland to Bristol and Aberdeen to Glentoran. However, Plymouth was confirmed as the venue, with the match being shown live on closed circuit TV at Old Trafford. The transmission of the match from Plymouth was a big improvement on the last closed circuit match at Old Trafford in 1969 against Milan. The BBC replayed the pictures from Home Park by land line and micro wave link to a receiving dish outside the ground, before being beamed onto six 30' x 40' screens. Although still in black and white, there was the benefit of action replays.

In 1977, the Executive Suite was extended with the opening of the Jubilee Room next to the Grill Room. This area saw the beginning of match sponsorship packages, with the sponsors and up to 50 guests receiving a champagne buffet prior to a match. On weekdays, the room was used for meetings, small exhibitions and private lunches.

With the club celebrating its centenary in 1978-79, a special match was arranged against old European rivals Read Madrid at the start of that particular season. It was decided by the board of directors that admission to all regular supporters would be free. Those to benefit from this decision would be all season ticket and League match ticket book holders, plus all other supporters who had between 18 and 22 programme tokens from the previous season. This was a kind gesture by the club, at a time when there wasn't exactly thousands in the bank.

The match itself was a nostalgic night, as members of past United teams filed onto the pitch prior to kick-off. Famous names such as Carey, Pearson, Rowley, Delaney, Blanchflower, Connelly and Charlton appeared on the park along with Jimmy Murphy and Sir Matt Busby, to warm applause from the 49,000 crowd. Representatives from every United Supporters Club also marched around the ground before the action got under way, with United making sure that their visitors did not spoil the party by winning 4-0. The goals came from Sammy McIlroy and Jimmy Greenhoff, each scoring two, and goalkeeper Alex Stepney saved a penalty.

During the close season, there had been little peace and quiet around the ground, with the constant noise of machinery as various improvements and alterations were carried out. The major work was carried out on the pitch by E.A.Yates and Sons of Sandbach, who set about trying to improve the drainage system. Three inch wide trenches were slit across the length and breadth of the pitch, to a depth of fourteen inches, and 230 tons of sand and gravel were injected in a bid to try and find a solution to what was once a quality playing surface. Elsewhere around the stadium additional safety barriers were erected, whilst the public address system was improved and now included the areas below the stands.

Safety was perhaps the main area of improvement with a police and fire control room being built, along with emergency lighting, a new fire alarm system, fire proofing of the snack bars and a better communication system all adding to better facilities, at a cost of £300,000. In October, at the clubs' AGM, plans were revealed for a £500,000 social club next to the ground. Negotiations were made with a brewery towards such a venture which it was hoped would rival that of Manchester City and also their Junior Blues set up. Chairman Louis Edwards said that the proposed club would feature a lounge room capable of holding between 500 and 600 people, and one of the objectives would be to invite parties from schools to come and watch films of United games. The initial idea was certainly welcomed by supporters, who were without any real form of a headquarters or match day meeting place, but it was some time before anything further was heard on the matter.

Unexpected refurbishing work had to be carried out on the Souvenir Shop, following a fire at the start of the season. Hundreds of pounds worth of stock was destroyed and the shop interior was severely damaged, causing the outlet to close. It was the end of September before it was re-opened, with investigations into the cause of the fire being carried out.

The dawn of the 1979-80 season saw further mention of the proposed social club, which was now called a supporters club. Chairman Louis Edwards announced the new plans while the club were abroad on their pre-season tour, and revealed that a new £1m extension would be built alongside the existing Executive Suite in the middle of the main stand, with the cantilever roofing extending round to the Stretford End. It would feature more private boxes with the main development providing rooms capable of holding almost 1,000 people and would be given over to the ordinary fans, with supporters club branches using the facilities on matchdays. With numerous branches from all over the country arriving at the ground early on matchdays, it was widely welcomed.

Upon returning from the pre-season tour of Germany and Denmark, the club staged a new venture at Old Trafford in the form of the first Open Day. This was attended by some 8,000 people and they watched trainer Tommy Cavanagh put the players through their paces, with bands, hot air balloons, police dog displays and other activities adding to the afternoons entertainment. Proceeds from the event went to the Variety Club Of Great Britain. The new £1m stand development, which involved the previously mentioned plans, was given the go ahead in October. This would double the accommodation of the existing suite, helping to reduce the extensive waiting list and also improve on the facilities. This announcement put shareholders attending the AGM a few days later in a happier mood, but did little to prepare them for a surprising revelation at the meeting.

Following an influx of new shareholders, which helped towards the club announcing record profits of £2m, more interest than ever before was paid to the AGM, with many of the new shareholders in attendance. One of these shareholders, a Mr Frank

Holt, a fervent supporter who at times seemed to have a weekly column in the Manchester Evening News Football Pink letters page, asked why the profits from the Souvenir Shop were not shown in the accounts. Chairman Louis Edwards replied that he could not answer that question, and amid shouts of *"why not"*, Sir Matt Busby stood up and said that the shop was, and always had been his, under Matt Busby Ltd, a private company.

Less than a couple of months after announcing their ambitious plans for the £1m redevelopment, incorporating the new supporters club, the Trafford Council Planning Committee blew the whistle on the idea by turning down the planning application. This was due to numerous complaints by residents living nearby who thought that the new club would bring trouble from rowdy supporters. One Councillor claimed that since the executive suite had been built, there had on occasions been trouble and the new venture would give youngsters the opportunity to obtain drink and cause further trouble. A noise problem and litter problem would also add to the residents worries, in Railway Road and Warwick Road. The councillor went on to suggest that the club should build on the opposite side of the ground away from the residential properties. United counterclaimed that there had been no trouble since the executive suite was opened and they would certainly protest against the decision.

The club came under further fire from the Trafford Planning Committee when it was claimed that they had begun work on their new development without receiving the necessary permission. Their reply was that they had only been having some work carried out on the drainage system! United then proceeded to submit amended plans which would give a better view to some 3,000 spectators, a new restaurant and lounge for 350 people, and a buffet room for entertaining supporters clubs. After much debate, the new plans received the go ahead and work could begin. The only remaining doubt seemed to be regarding the television reception in surrounding homes and the club agreed to ensure, at their own expense, that there would be no interference and they would give written assurances regarding this as well as on the subject of crowd control.

The redevelopment of the ground was all very well, but a more pressing necessity was the pitch during the winter weather, when games were postponed due to it being frozen. Numerous matches had been called off over the years and cries had gone out time and time again for undersoil heating or whatever, but the club had always pushed all considerations to the side, preferring nature just to take its course. It was now felt, however, that it was time to do something, and a special study was set up in the hope that a system could be found that would not endanger the playing surface.

On Monday February 26th 1980, Mr Louis Edwards, the club chairman, died at his home in Alderley Edge Cheshire. He had recently been the subject of an ITV 'World In Action' programme - 'The Man Who Bought United', and the club had come under the spotlight for all the wrong reasons following the broadcast. Since he became a director, and chairman in 1965, he had played a major part in transforming Old Trafford into the 'Wembley Of The North', and following his retirement from his meat business he had been an almost daily visitor to the ground and had recently moved into a newly built office beside the executive suite. His ambition had always been to generate the same sort of income through off the field activities as that which came through the turnstiles, and who was to say that he would not have succeeded?

March 22nd marked the date of the 100th Manchester 'Derby' match, and prior to the kick-off it was announced that Martin Edwards was to succeed his father as club chairman. His first appearance as chairman was soon to follow, when along with his City counterpart, Peter Swales, they walked onto the pitch to exchange gifts. As for the match itself, it was only memorable for the occasion, with the record books showing a 1-0 United victory. Neither side had scored in their previous three games, so the pre-match prospects of an outstanding match were rather dim. United goalkeeper Bailey was troubled only a couple of times in the entire first-half, while at the opposite end there was little more activity, with a Thomas shot bringing out the best in Corrigan.

The second forty-five minutes, however, began with a bang. Jordan found McIlroy on the left. He in turn moved the ball wide to Albiston, who in turn pushed it on to Thomas moving into the penalty area. The quick shot from the little Welshman struck Henry on the toe and spiralled over the helpless City 'keeper into the net. One nil to United, and that was it really. City did try and press forward, but they just did not have the players to break down the United defence, who on the other hand failed to take control and continually gave the ball away, much to the home crowd's disappointment and annoyance. The remainder of the game produced little and the 100th 'derby' match would be remembered simply as just another match (and victory) against City.

Fixtures against Manchester City are always high profile affairs attracting capacity crowds, with this latest being watched by 56,387. But such attendances at Old Trafford are nothing out of the ordinary and therefore each fixture is well policed as a major operation is put in force. Policing Old Trafford around 25 times per season was an expensive business, costing United a minimum £3,700 a match for crowd control, with the tax-payer having to pay out another £2,600 towards traffic control and street patrols.

The whole match day operation was run by a chief superintendent who had everything at the ground, except the directors lounge, at his disposal. The Old Trafford layout, with its fencing and small manageable paddocks helped make crowd control a little easier, but from the mouth of the players tunnel he controlled his 120 or so officers around the ground, (who would be earning £14-39p less tax for their four hour shift), with an exercise of tact and experienced organisation.

The officers worked in commando type units, in positions where they could see and be seen clearly. One would be on the roof with binoculars while in close communication through radio with others, while outside the stadium foot patrols, mounted police, and dog patrols would escort opposition supporters from their coaches down by the cricket ground up Warwick Road, keeping United infiltrators at bay. A similar operation was carried out at full-time.

The Stretford End, once the nerve centre of the United support, didn't cause as much trouble as it used to, with troublemakers having moved into the Paddocks at the opposite end, to be nearer to the opposition fans, where they could exchange insults and throw items such as coins, bolts and the occasional dart. With the Old Trafford crowds being larger and at that time potentially more violent, the success of the police operations were shown by the average of only one and a half arrests per match.

It had been some time since an International fixture had been played at Old Trafford, but with season 1980-81 only a couple of months old the England 'B' team faced the United States under the floodlights. It was the first visit to this country by the U.S. national side since the 1948 Olympic Games and they put up a spirited performance, losing only 1-0 to a strong England XI, with United's 22 year old goalkeeper, Gary Bailey, in the side.

Building work was progressing on the new extension to the executive suite and on the afternoon of December 13th, for the match against Stoke City, the £1.5m development was opened. It now enabled over 700 members, each paying £360 plus VAT per season, to enjoy the dining and wining facilities along with a special seat in the stand to watch the game.

The stand roof had been further cantilevered, with the old roof support pillars removed as part of the ground development. This now gave Old Trafford five specialist function rooms - the Grill Room, Stretford Suite, Trafford Suite, Europa Suite and Jubilee Room.

The first mentioned, which was situated on the ground floor of the complex, was open weekdays, 12-2.30 and on home match days, but then only available to executive suite members, until 6.30. The Stretford, on the upper floor of the new extension to the restaurant complex offered an a-la-carte menu with window tables overlooking the pitch. The Trafford, situated above the Grill Room, again had window seating with the additional attraction of an impressive showcase of club trophies and mementoes. This was mainly an evening function room and could be adapted to hold two at the same time. The Europa, the latest addition, was possibly the most versatile, and was

The main frontage in 1981

used by the Development Association agents on matchdays. Finally, the Jubilee Room, adjacent to the Grill Room, was used on matchdays by sponsors and doubled for a small function room for special occasions. Further alterations at the end of the season actually brought people swarming to the ground and they all went home happy without seeing a ball being kicked or any of the United players.

It was decided by the club to rip up the pitch, taking off the top six inches of soil and then work in around 1,200 tons of sand before preparing a seed bed and sowing new grass. The scheme would cost around £40,000, but it was hoped it would create a much better playing surface and improve the drainage system. It was the first time for 20 years that the pitch had been completely torn up.

Word soon got round that the turf was being dug up and piled outside the ground. In next to no time, cars and vans began appearing with eager supporters filling plastic bags with sections of the hallowed turf to take home and relay in their gardens. Some were happy with a mere square of turf, while one fan from Timperley completely replaced his lawn, and incorporated the penalty spot!

The playing surface soon returned to normal, much to everyones relief, but on the 17th September 1981, minor adjustments were made to the pitch markings, goal posts removed and black sight screens were installed. Cricket had moved a few hundred yards up the Warwick Road from one Old Trafford to the other. Just over 3,000 spectators paid to watch the Lambert and Butler seven-a-side tournament, with Lancashire taking on Yorkshire, and Nottinghamshire facing Derbyshire. The two winners then faced each other for the right to play in the Final of the competition at Stamford Bridge.

Under the lights, with yellow pads and a white ball, it was the likes of Clive Lloyd and Graeme Fowler instead of Coppell and Wilkins being cheered on, with Nottinghamshire and Lancashire competing against each other in the 10 overs, one innings, decider. At the end of the evening it was the 'local' team that went on to the Final in London. Football, tennis, rugby, cricket....what would be next?

With the success of the Family Open Days, the third having been held in the summer, it was decided to begin behind the scenes tours of the stadium, as such things were impossible to attempt on the open days due to the numbers attracted. A tour guide was appointed and supporters could book their tour on any day except Sunday (and of course matchday). With supporters always on the look out for something different, they were quick to take advantage of this new feature.

Spectators at the ground on Saturday October 3rd 1981 for the match against Wolverhampton Wanderers also witnessed something a little different with the signing of a player on the pitch before the kick-off. Usually something that was carried out in the confines of the chairman's office, with the press sometimes in attendance, West Bromwich Albion's midfielder Bryan Robson sat at a table in front of the main stand to sign a contract which made him a United player for a fee of £1.7m. His signing had an immediate effect on the man he was widely tipped to replace, Sammy McIlroy. The Irishman proved to everyone that he had no intentions of being the man to make way for the new signing by scoring a memorable hat trick in a 5-0 victory. The other United goals came from Stapleton and Birtles in what was at times a stunning display of football.

The cost of watching football will always be debated, with prices seemingly ever-increasing and United taking as much criticism as anyone. However, Wednesday November 4th saw the gates at Old Trafford thrown open to anyone who cared to come along and watch a United XI play Sydney Olympic in a friendly fixture. The reason for the free admission was due to the fact that United were unsure how many people would turn up for the 2pm kick-off and the expense of gatemen might not be justified. Schoolmasters and employers were the only ones to complain and around 3,000 attended the match which United won 2-1.

The call for undersoil heating had been echoing around the ground for a few years now, and following another winter of postponed fixtures, Chairman Martin Edwards finally announced that the board were to discuss the installation of a system. With the complete overhaul of the pitch during the previous summer, it was now felt that things could be taken a step further as the playing surface was now in excellent condition. Money for such a venture would be no problem as attendances were excellent, with the 'derby' match against City on February 27th attracting 57,872 and most of the previous fixtures achieving figures of around 45,000 or more.

United soon released plans for a rock concert at the ground, which could bring them profits of around £50,000, but in the end all it brought was a lot of complaints and the club considering what might have been. The concert had been pencilled in for Saturday May 29th and was to feature Queen.

A crowd of some 46,000 would have been expected, with the gates opening around 9am and music from a DJ beginning at 2pm. Two support bands would be playing from 4.30pm, with Queen taking the stage in the evening, and finishing at 10pm. However, all the plans were hit on the head by Trafford Council who refused to grant the club an entertainment license due to the noise and nuisance the concert would cause local residents. United protested against the decision, but to no avail and the concert was switched to Elland Road Leeds much to the locals delight and United's dismay.

The only market that United had ever had any interest in was the transfer one, but with running a football club becoming more and more a business, any source of income was worth considering, as the ill-fated concert had shown. A company called Kavanger approached the club with the suggestion of holding Sunday Markets in one of the large car parks adjacent to the ground, and United showed an interest due to the financial gain they could obtain. Like the concert, plans were drawn up and it was announced that from Sunday October 3rd 1982, between 9am and 2pm there would be 100's of stalls in the main car park selling a wide variety of goods and that it would become a regular occurrence. Much to Kavanger and United's dismay, however, it was not to be so easy. Both Manchester City Council and Trafford District Council opposed the plans and twenty-four hours before the scheme was due to take off, an injunction was brought out against it. United and Kavanger could have pursued the matter further, but after much discussion it was agreed to forget about the whole idea.

On Saturday February 12th 1983, when thousands of supporters should have been at the ground for the match against Luton Town and to remember those who had lost their lives at Munich twenty five-years previously, the ground stood empty as once again heavy frost brought the postponement of yet another fixture. Again the cries of complaint were heard, and once again the Chairman made the excuses. He said that the club had a duty to the supporters and pointed out the dangers of having them travel along snow bound roads and streets and then having to stand on slippery terracing.

On that particular Saturday, however, the Old Trafford pitch was the only area of Manchester affected by the cold snap. Why could a club with such healthy finances not invest in some type of ground heating while a few miles up the road Oldham Athletic had often felt the benefit of having installed undersoil heating in the summer of 1981?

United came under fire again a couple of weeks later, following the fixture against Liverpool of February 26th. With the teams holding the top places in the First Division and also Milk Cup Finalists, many were surprised that the match was not an all-ticket affair. United, however, explained that when the decision was made, the average attendance at Old Trafford was around 40,000 and Liverpool were only expected to bring between 2 and 3,000, which would leave a margin of 15,000 before the capacity would be reached. This was considered enough to keep the game a 'pay at the turnstile one'.

On matchday it was found to be a big mistake, as interest had grown, and as kick-off approached the scenes outside the ground brought howls of protest. The gates had to be shut some 45 minutes before the start, with thousands still outside and ugly scenes developing. Children and adults were crushed, with other collapsing due to the pressure of those behind trying to reach the already locked gates. Control was in total disarray with the mounted police being unable to restore immediate calm. Fighting also broke out as tempers became frayed. With a club such as United having such good organisation, scenes like this should have been easy to avoid. Inside the ground there was an attendance of 57,397 and a crowd the size of an average Third Division match outside listening to the noise from the game that produced a 1-1 draw.

Following the F.A. Cup success against Brighton and an F.A. Charity Shield victory over Liverpool at the start of 1983-84, the new campaign, with the treat of European football once again at Old Trafford was eagerly looked forward to.

During the summer, around £800,000 had been spent on various sections of the stadium, with everyone from the ordinary fan on the terracing to those fortunate enough to be Executive Suite members able to enjoy improved facilities. The latter were now given a view overlooking the pitch from the bar and dining room following a re-arrangement of the restaurant. A further £100,000 was earmarked for future improvement of this section. Catering facilities were also improved around the stadium, with the 20 sites receiving a facelift over a two year period at a cost of £150,000. New caterers were to be employed and a bigger and better variety of food and refreshments would be available on matchdays. The private boxes, an important part of the club's revenue, were also in line for improvement at a cost of £500,000.

One scheme originally planned (at long last), the installation of undersoil heading, had to be temporarily postponed due to the £80,000 drainage system leaving the grass little time to develop. The £60,000 heating system was to be the main project for the following summer, although it was disappointing to see it put back a year. To be fair, however, if the club had gone ahead with it as planned it would have caused problems with the playing surface in the immediate months ahead.

Early September saw the club stage a successful Open Day at the ground, with around 15,000 turning up for the charity fund raising event. Queues for a tour behind the scenes, at 50p a time, stretched back over the Warwick Road railway bridge, while more than 2,000 supporters paid £1 to have their photograph taken with the F.A. Cup.

The day incorporated a five mile fun run, in which Chairman Martin Edwards took part, and should have seen the ground close at 5pm, but it was nearer to 8.30pm before the last of the fans made their way home.

The amount raised for charity through the Open Day was minute compared with the sum that the club expected to earn during the months ahead, as a new League ruling now allowed the home side to keep all the money they took through the turnstiles, making a gate of 42,000 worth around £105,000 to United. With their involvement in three cup competitions added to the League fixtures, a figure of well over £3 million could be pulled in. The business side of the club was now becoming even more important, and the previously ill-fated

Sunday Market finally began operation for a short while with around 70 stalls present. Early in 1984 Martin Edwards announced that he had agreed in principle to staging an American Grid Iron football match at Old Trafford, *"If the teams are right and provided we can get permission from the local council. If it doesn't go ahead this summer, then perhaps next"*. It was hoped to bring together the Los Angeles Raiders and Dallas Cowboys, but whether anything further would develop was open to debate and as with numerous ideas in the past, nothing more was heard.

Friday December 16th, was another date for the United history books, with the first live television showing of a League match from Old Trafford. The fixture, against Tottenham Hotspur was shown on BBC between 7.05 and 9.00 and was presented by Jimmy Hill with John Motson the match commentator. Not only was it shown live in England, but the Scottish BBC also showed it along with Italy and Poland. Highlights were to be shown in at least another 40 countries, adding up to the biggest worldwide audience for an English League match.

The game itself, a thrilling 4-2 victory for United with goals from Arthur Graham and Kevin Moran netting two apiece, with Brazil and Falco scoring for Spurs, only attracted 33,616 spectators, forcing the Football League to pay United compensation of around £50,000 for loss of revenue, as a 50,000 gate could normally have been expected for this fixture.

In the early weeks of 1983, the Old Trafford action drifted from the pitch to the board room, with talks of a takeover beginning to drift around Manchester. A £10 million figure was put on the club as millionaire publisher Robert Maxwell moved to the forefront of the take over deal. Cheap at the price? His £10 million deal would bring him control of the club which began in a six shillings a week rented cottage with a handful of players and staff, and now the splendid surroundings of Old Trafford to call home, incorporating 8 chefs, 27 catering staff, 27 workers in the development association office, 20 in the club administration, 6 stadium crew plus players and management, along with a £70,000 a year rates bill. There was also the lure of a thriving commercial side, which had declared

a trading profit of £600,000 the previous year. The takeover soon snowballed and began to attract more newspaper coverage than the teams exploits on the pitch, as the price began to creep up towards the £15 million mark. In the end, Chairman Martin Edwards remained in charge and all thoughts of selling were soon forgotten as a European date with Spanish giants Barcelona loomed on the horizon.

The visit to the Nou Camp stadium in Barcelona on the evening of March 7th left United with a 2-0 deficiency to make up in the return leg at Old Trafford. Although they had not been outclassed, an own goal by Graeme Hogg in his first European appearance and a last minute goal from Rojo gave United plenty to think about on the journey home. In the Manchester Evening News the following day, their United correspondent David Meek seemed to sum it all up by writing that *"United need a football miracle if they are to reach the semi-finals of the European Cup Winners Cup"*.

A fortnight later, a 58,350 full house at Old Trafford witnessed one of those magical European nights, conjuring up an atmosphere that can only be created at a midweek game under the floodlights. Paying record receipts of almost £200,000, the crowd were certainly given value for money as the game bubbled into life right from the kick-off. As early as the 15th minute, United had the Barcelona goal under pressure, when Whiteside, reacting quickly to a mix up between Urruti and Alexanco on the edge of their penalty area, hit the top of the bar with a neat lob which ended up on the roof of the unguarded net.

With Remi Moses keeping a close watch on Argentinian dangerman Maradona, Schuster and Victor poised the biggest threat to the home defence, but Moran and Hogg stood firm to anything that came their way. United got the opening they were looking for in the 22nd minute, following a corner won by Stapleton. Taken by Wilkins, it was headed on by Whiteside and Bryan Robson headed past Urruti from close range, sending the crowd wild.

Wilkins should have done better with a shot after 35 minutes, but put it wide from 15 yards out, while a counter-attack by Barcelona saw Marcos also driving wide, and shortly after Bailey saved well from Maradona as the Spaniards searched for the equaliser. As the half-time whistle blew the score remained 2-1 to Barcelona on aggregate, leaving the crowd a short period to regain their breath and contemplate the exciting 45 minutes ahead.

Within seven minutes of the restart, United were 3-0 ahead on the night and now held the aggregate advantage, through a second goal by Robson and one from Stapleton. In the 50th minute, a back pass by Alonso created problems and allowed Moses to centre from the right. A shot from Wilkins was fumbled by the Barcelona 'keeper and Robson gratefully accepted a close range opportunity to level the scores on aggregate. Two minutes later, a stunned Barcelona found themselves further behind. Albiston's penetrating run and cross was headed goalwards by Whiteside, and Stapleton, lurking at the far post, sent the ball past Urruti in front of a rapturous Stretford End.

The volume of noise rose to a crescendo as the game went into overdrive. Schuster was booked for a foul on Wilkins, Bailey pulled off a couple of excellent saves, while at the other end Robson once again came close to scoring. United, however, held on and as the final whistle blew, sections of the crowd spilled onto the pitch to salute their heroes. Most of the players managed to find the sanctuary of the dressing rooms without too much of a problem, but the hero of the evening, Bryan Robson, was lifted shoulder high and carried from the field of play by the United supporters. Unfortunately, hopes of glory in Europe were dashed in the semi-finals by Juventus, who reached the Final with a 3-2 aggregate win.

November 1984 saw plans put before the Trafford Borough Council's Planning Committee to re-develop the old Scoreboard Paddock section of the ground. This project, which would create stand L, would provide a further 1800 seats and 15 executive boxes inside the stadium, with a new ticket office on the outside. It was also hoped to incorporate a form of club museum in this section, but the plans were still at a very early stage.

An ideal quiz question for the future was conjured up during season 1984-85 - "Which European tie at Old Trafford did United not play in?" - came about on December 12th, when Glasgow Celtic played Rapid Vienna in a highly controversial ECWC 2nd round leg tie. Following dramatic scenes in the original 2nd leg tie at Parkhead, Celtic were ordered to replay the game, which they had won 3-0 (4-3 on aggregate), at a neutral venue a certain distance from Glasgow, with Old Trafford being selected. Further controversy loomed. Around 50,000 Scottish invaders took over the ground, (and indeed Manchester itself), but many brought disgrace to the Glasgow club and its vast majority of well behaved supporters, who had in the past enjoyed testimonial games at Old Trafford.

Trailing 1-0 on the night, and 4-1 on aggregate, trouble flared in the 63rd minute, shortly after a penalty claim for a foul on Brian McClair had been turned down. A spectator managed to find his way onto the pitch and with play at the opposite end of the ground, punched the Austrian goalkeeper into the back of the net before Rapid players and six policemen intervened. As the minutes ticked away towards full-time, another fan encroached onto the pitch only to be tackled by five policemen, and with attention for the moment diverted, another fan found his way onto the pitch and managed to kick an Austrian player before being apprehended. It was later revealed that both assailants were in fact English based supporters.

Work soon began on the new ground development, following the passing of plans, causing a disruption to the running of the club and the supporters. Temporary measures had to be taken and the ticket office found new accommodation in the vicinity of K stand in what was the Supporters Club office, while the Souvenir Shop was also moved into temporary premises in the form of a large portacabin on the forecourt.

The Supporters Club office moved alongside the Development Office beside the railway, while a new site had to be found for the Munich clock. After much consideration, it was decided to put it on the wall of the lift tower at the front of the stadium.

As 1984 moved into 1985, with the 75th anniversary of the opening of the stadium drawing near, opinions were being voiced that the ground should be re-named 'Busby Stadium' after the man who had done so much for the club. The modest Sir Matt, however, would not have been too eager for such an innovation to be considered, as he was always content to have the three great teams he created as his memorial. The suggestion had reached the ears of the United directors and had been carefully noted. Although they did not go as far as agreeing to the opinions, they pleased everyone, including Sir Matt, by commissioning a bust of the great man, which would proudly stand at the entrance to the planned museum, scheduled to be opened at the ground the next season.

In addition, a Sir Matt Busby Suite would be incorporated into the new stand construction on the Warwick Road end of the ground. This suite would be for the ordinary supporters on matchdays and would be able to accommodate 300 people.

The early rounds of the F.A. Cup inadvertently produced numerous upsets and red faces amongst the 'big names' of the top division. The third round of the 1985 competition almost brought embarrassment to United, without a ball being kicked. Having pondered with the installation of undersoil heating for so long and finally going ahead and doing so during the summer, the winter temperatures should have created little problem for Old Trafford. However, the system's 'debut' prior to the third round tie against Bournemouth on January 5th almost caused much embarrassment.

The thermostats proved faulty and had to be replaced on the Thursday, leaving a couple of 60 yard sections of the pitch to be thawed out in a short period of time, with heavy overnight frost also being forecast. On Friday, the match referee, a Mr Brazier from Northampton, decided the pitch was unplayable in parts, but agreed to leave the final decision until 10.15 on the Saturday morning. Thankfully the red faces (and the wrath of the travelling supporters) were spared and at the end of the day the heating system had caused more problems than the Third Division opposition, with United winning 3-0.

The 49,443 spectators who arrived at the ground for the opening fixture of season 1985-86, against Aston Villa, saw the further development of the ground for the first time. New seating had been installed in stands A,B,C, and D, with a few of the 40 year old wooden seats finding their way to new homes as supporters prized a few away for souvenirs as they lay outside the ground during the installation. At one point, it looked as though they might be asked to return them, as the installation of the new seats fell a little behind schedule, with the last of the new seats being screwed into place a mere hour before the Villa match. Incorporated into the new stand L was a 'Family Stand', exclusively for the use of families with adults only gaining admission if accompanied by a child.

Thursday August 29th saw Sir Matt officially open the new suite named after him. This facility, housed on ground level at the front of the new stand, was the first phase of the 'United Visitors Centre'. It's luxurious surroundings provided the supporter with a fine range of food and drink as well as an ideal meeting place, although to begin with it was restricted to Development Agents only. One of the unique features of the suite was a magnificent mural along one wall, painted by local artist Walter Kershaw. The 30ft long mural depicted the history of United from the Newton Heath days right through to the previous season's F.A. Cup winning goal by Norman Whiteside against Everton.

Re-developing the ground with its Europa, Stretford, Trafford and Warwick suites and other excellent facilities, along with the changing faces of playing personnel, gave the impression that the club had a bottomless purse. However, as football in general began to feel something of a tug on its purse strings, United decided that after spending £2.5 million on the ground and a European ban on British clubs', following the Hysel Stadium disaster the previous season, a close watch had to be kept on the financial situation at the club, forcing them to shelve an ambitious scheme to build a £3 million 8,000 seater sports hall beside the ground. The clubs' adoption of a basketball team played a big part in the original idea of such a venue, but Chairman Martin Edwards decided that an indoor complex was something that could be done without at present.

The Hysel tragedy not only saw the loss of revenue from European fixtures hit the pocket of United and others, but the subsequent banning of alcohol at grounds also created a decrease in revenue. The law, banning the sale of alcohol at points which overlooked the pitch, prompted United to raise the matter with Trafford magistrates, as the main bars at the ground were out of sight of the playing area and as long as the supporters drank at them it was felt that there was no problem.

The success on the field, with the club hitting their seventh straight win of the season against Oxford United, seemed to boost affairs off the pitch with the club successful in its appeal to serve alcohol at the 29 bars scattered around the stadium on match days. Worth around £500,000 a year in income, it was a welcome result, but it was not a 100% victory as a ban remained on a bar in the main stand overlooking the pitch and also in two 250 seater restaurants with similar viewing facilities. The magistrates granted an application to the club to serve drinks for the hours prior to home matches and in some executive areas for an hour after evening games. It was also good news for 50 of the catering staff who had earlier lost their jobs due to the ban, for they would now be re-instated.

League, F.A. Cup, Football League Cup and various European competitions had been contested at Old Trafford in the past, but on September 18th came yet another first with a Match against Everton in the newly created Football League Super Cup. Unfortunately the outstanding League form, (which had now stretched to eight straight wins), stuttered on the night and the Goodison Park side recorded a 4-2 victory.

As the winter nights began to close in, the evening sky around the ground was lit up a little brighter from November 16th, by a new 'Manchester United' neon sign on the cantilever roof above what was once the Old Trafford Paddock section of the ground. The cantilever roof, previously referred to, now extended around three quarters of the stadium providing an uninterrupted view for spectators in those sections. Just around the corner from the new neon sign a completely new main entrance with a reception area had been included as part of the new office complex which straddled the road around the ground on the railway side.

For United officials and supporters it was not entirely a satisfactory start to 1986, as a similar situation occurred to that of twelve months previously, with the undersoil heating system failing to live up to its expectations. On the Friday afternoon, prior to the January 4th third round F.A. Cup-tie against near neighbours Rochdale, it became noticeable that the system was not functioning properly. Cold overnight weather did not help the situation and a 9am Saturday morning inspection brought little hope of the game taking place. A further inspection two hours later brought the expected 'match off' announcement. A team of experts dug up part of the pitch in a major investigation and discovered that part of the ultra-modern protection was corroded or burnt out, only fifteen months after it was installed.

Plans for a United Museum had been revealed some time ago, but in the club programme the 'United Review' for February 22nd 1986, supporters were given their first look at the plans and in the following five issues an artist's impression of how the concept might look was included. Since the idea was first mentioned, numerous items had been handed in to swell the already large collection of trophies and memorabilia assembled by the club over the years. Obviously there would not be enough room to display everything, but the showcases in the museum would cover the complete history of the club from the days as Newton Heath to the present, and would include everything from shirts and contracts to medals and match tickets.

Inter-active displays featuring videos and computers were early suggestions for sections of the museum, but the sheer volume of items made this impractical if as much as possible was going to be displayed. The Aladdin's cave of United memorabilia was eagerly awaited by those supporters who could not get enough of the club.

The doors of the museum, situated above the Sir Matt Busby Suite, eventually opened on Thursday May 1st 1986, when club President Sir Matt Busby, along with local civic dignitaries, present and former players, plus other special guests (including Duncan Edwards' mother) watched club Chairman Martin Edwards cut the ribbon on the £100,000 development, originally suggested by the late director Denzil Haroun.

As season 1986-87 got underway, the home match against Charlton Athletic, on August 30th, saw the official opening of the Family Stand by F.A. Chairman Mr Bert Millerchip, who was accompanied by F.A. Secretary Ted Croker and Graham Kelly the Secretary of the Football League. At a time when hooliganism was still causing a problem, it was a notable move by United to promote good feeling between young supporters, with families of visiting clubs often receiving an allocation of tickets. Old Trafford was already one of the safest grounds in the country, thanks to excellent police supervision and segregation.

How often new goal posts have been installed at Old Trafford there is no record, but on October 25th 1986, the posts were altered to accommodate enthusiasts of the oval ball for the Whitbread Trophy Bitter 1st Rugby League Test between Great Britain and Australia. The prestigious event had captured the imagination of the Rugby League world and the BBC considered it important enough to broadcast their 'Grandstand' programme live from one of the luxury boxes at the ground, while their Radio Two counterparts used the box next door. Unfortunately the weather did not match the occasion, but a crowd of 50,583 (with many other locked out) braved the elements to watch.

A week prior to the rugby fixture, Luton Town's League visit to Old Trafford saw the new floodlighting system being switched on for part of the match. The first full match played under the new lights was a Littlewoods Cup-tie against Southampton on October 20th. Gone were the pylons, landmarks eagerly looked out for by those travelling to the ground for the first time, which had been erected in 1957. In their place were 216 fittings, with 2500 watt lamps, situated along the roofs of both touchline stands. Costing around £170,000 (not including the dismantling of the old lights), compared with £40,000 for the old 1957 version, the Thorn EMI system took just over five months to be installed by contractors Piggot and Whitfield of Stockport.

The F.A. Cup once again brought the cold weather, and the continued disappointment of the undersoil heating failing to live up to its expectations. In place for less than three years, the board decided

that enough was enough and that it would be ripped out during the coming summer, but thankfully the threatened Cup-tie went ahead as it was no ordinary third round match, but a local 'derby' against Manchester City. Manager Alex Ferguson's first Cup-tie in the United hot-seat was only saved from embarrassment with the hire of a line of industrial hot air heaters, which pumped hot air onto the frozen areas of the playing surface.

April 1987 brought a significant announcement from Chairman Martin Edwards, and one which would change the matchday arrangements of many supporters, with the introduction of a club membership scheme. United were the first to react on a government demand for football clubs to have greater control over their own supporters and the following season would see the introduction of a members only scheme for supporters wishing to watch games from either the Stretford End or the United Road Paddock.

The proposed scheme would cost £5 to join, but there would be additional benefits such as reduced admission to League games, priority cup tickets and discount souvenirs. The need for membership would also apply to Season Ticket and League Match Ticket book holders in both sections.

With the ground capacity then standing at 56,000, the membership scheme would initially attract around 28,000, but it was hoped that the other sections of the ground, which were available to non-members and visiting supporters, might also become members only areas. This season had only seen five arrests at the ground, so trouble prevention certainly wasn't the motive behind the introduction of the scheme, which was not received too favourably by a large majority of the supporters.

During the close season, the newly established membership office at the ground was kept busy with around 200 applications per day, as supporters not wanting to find themselves locked out of the ground once the season got under way, eagerly parted with their £5.

With Arsenal as the first visitors to Old Trafford for season 1987-88, a side who regularly produce one of the better fixtures each season, the

Manchester Evening News' United correspondent David Meek wrote on the day of the match that he hoped that, *"United supporters had got the message that it was members only in the Stretford End and United Road Paddock, or there could be chaotic scenes outside the ground"*. In an attempt to avoid this problem, United had the membership office open prior to the match and also a portacabin in the forecourt for supporters wishing to join on the night. However, such warnings went unheeded, with hundreds still queuing at the turnstiles when United kicked off, many of whom were not members. The Stretford End caused the biggest problem.

Following the match, United claimed that they had everyone inside the ground by 8pm, half an hour after the kick-off, but by then many had given up all hope of gaining entry and gone home. The attendance was only 42,890, well below the expected 50,000, and numerous complaints were made to the club, but thankfully the early teething problems were overcome and supporters realised that the membership scheme was here to stay.

Brian McClair from Celtic was one of the summer signings, but the work of Sauters of Stirling had the ability to turn just as important. The Scottish company laid a completely new surface on the pitch with the installation of 20 miles of plastic piping 10 inches below the surface, providing what was hoped to be the perfect undersoil heating system at long last.

Spectators in the Stretford End section of the ground would enjoy the benefit of improved facilities in the months ahead, while £50,000 had been spent by the ground caterers Letheby and Christopher on the all round improvement of their services.

A 1-1 televised match against Liverpool on November 15th provided the normal fever pitched atmosphere, but it also produced some severe after match comments from the visiting goalkeeper Bruce Grobbelaar, who claimed that he was subjected to an endless stream of missiles for forty-five minutes of the match. Everything from eggs, coins and bananas had been thrown into his goalmouth. Fortunately for the club no action was taken, nor were the Liverpool 'keepers suggestions

that large perspex screens should be erected at the Stretford End to protect all visiting custodians. The Liverpool match also created something of a record on the catering side, with 864 meals served on the day!

Three days later, United had the unusual situation of playing an away match at home. The 4th round draw for the Littlewoods Cup paired the club with Bury at Gigg Lane, but the near neighbours felt that it would be more profitable to switch the tie to Old Trafford. This fixture also produced the first senior football match at the ground when the United Review was not on sale for a United game, as Bury produced 35,000 of their own programmes to be sold on the night. For the record, United won 2-1, away at home.

While mentioning the United Review, an interesting item appeared in the issue for the match against Oxford United on December 12th, when an article revealed that the United Executive Suite had recently completed its largest single function since the opening in 1975. The event, held by the Electrical Contractors Association, was a two day exhibition in the Europa and Trafford Suites, with the Warwick Suite and private boxes used for catering. Some 2,125 meals were served.

Giant Sumo wrestlers, jugglers and other forms of entertainment took over the ground on the 15th May 1988 when, for the second season running, the Rugby League Premiership Finals were held there. Extended posts and the oval ball were becoming regular accessories to the Old Trafford equipment stores.

With the summer of 1988 on the way, there were no ground developments planned, as it was considered much more important and productive to improve the playing side and any cash should be made available to the manager for such matters.

Midway through season 1988-89, the government began to make it known that they felt strongly regarding the introduction of an ID card for all football supporters, a move that United were very much against. So strongly did United feel about the matter, that they produced a detailed brochure - 'Football: National Membership Scheme. A United Perspective'. This publication explained the club policy regarding crowd control etc. and included much in the way of interesting information. Appendix B for instance, showed a chart which detailed the flow of spectators through the turnstiles for an evening match, with the Sheffield Wednesday fixture on November 23rd taken as the example. For the 7.30pm kick off, the gates opened at 6.30 with 2% entering between then and 6.45, followed by 14% in the next five minutes. Surprisingly, 10% passed through the turnstiles between 7.30 and 7.35!

Appendix C showed a detailed season by season list of ejections and arrests compared with the average attendances between 1978-79 and ,1987-88. 9,217,994 people passed through the turnstiles in those seasons, with a total of 752 arrests and 2,034 ejected. The season which showed the highest figure was 1978-79, with 430 and 152 respectively. What the final outcome regarding the introduction of ID cards at this particular time was anyones guess.

With no alterations to the stadium structure during 1988-89, events which took place at the ground can be looked at more closely during this period. At the beginning of April, United announced that they planned to hold a Pop Concert on July 18th, with American stars Daryl Hall and John Oates as the main act. If they were not available then replacements such as Womack and Womack or Chris Rea would be approached.

The United commercial manager explained that it was an ideal way to bring in some revenue during the close season, but everything would hinge on the local residents supporting the plans, as previous attempts to hold a concert had always fallen through due to the local opposition. Once again, however, the residents in the vicinity of the stadium overcame United's challenge and the concert became a non-event.

For the second time in recent seasons, tragedy struck at an English club stadium. On May 11th 1985, 56 people died and around 200 were injured as fire swept through the main stand at Bradford City's Valley Parade ground during their Third Division match against Lincoln City. Prior to the match, the 3,500 to 4,000 spectators who were in the old wooden stand had been in a party mood

celebrating Bradford's promotion to the Second Division, but the fire spoiled not only their celebrations but also the rest of the their lives.

On Saturday April 15th 1989, disaster struck at Sheffield Wednesday's Hillsborough ground not long after the start of the F.A. Cup Semi-Final tie between Nottingham Forest and Liverpool, producing events that the thousands who attend football matches every week up and down the country never give a moments thought to. At the Leppings Lane end of the ground, (an area occupied by United supporters on several similar occasions in the past), where the Liverpool contingent were massed, a late surge of supporters, determined not to miss much of the action pressed towards the gates.

Such was the pressure on the exit gates beside the turnstiles that a senior police officer felt it safer to open them, even though it allowed many without tickets to gain entry. This resulted in a massive tide of bodies pushing into those already congregated on the terracing watching the opening minutes of the game.

The steel perimeter fencing, familiar at many grounds (but missing from Bradford's Valley Parade thus saving many lives due to the easy access onto the pitch) prevented those at the front of the terracing from escaping the crush. Many were trampled underfoot in the chaos that followed, and at the end of the day a total of 94 died and a further 170 were injured.

Could such a disaster ever occur at Old Trafford? It is easy to write no, but one can never tell what might happen, but with the layout of the stadium it would be extremely doubtful. With 29 safety gates around the perimeter fencing, access onto the pitch is at hand for every section. The Scoreboard End, with a capacity for 4,500 standing spectators, was divided into two sections, each with its separate entrance and exits with stewards and police well in control. At the opposite end of the ground, the Stretford End with an 8,700 capacity, there is one large tunnel behind the goal, but with additional access and turnstiles at one of the sides. Control of the crowd is monitored from a police operations room, while the club has its own control point with computers registering the number of people in each section of the ground.

With the fateful Semi-Final still to be played, Old Trafford was selected as the new venue, a popular choice with both competing clubs, as it had already been chosen as a venue for any required replay. So, Saturday April 29th saw Liverpool face Forest in the F.A. Cup, which resulted in the Merseyside club marching to Wembley on a wave of emotion to face local rivals Everton in the Final.

Merseyside had already triumphed at Old Trafford the week prior to the F.A. Cup match when Leasowe Pacific defeated Friends Of Fulham 3-2 in the Womans F.A. Cup Final. A meagre crowd of around 1,000 watched the match, which some of those present said produced the best ninety minutes football seen at the ground all season.

It was something of a busy spell for the United ground staff, with the two fixtures just mentioned, together with United's first and second team League games, a Schoolboy International (between England and Scotland), an English Schools' Trophy Semi-Final between Salford and Plymouth, and the subsequent Final between Salford and St. Helens, as well as the Rugby League Premiership Finals.

While mentioning the above schoolboy games, it is worth nothing that a youngster by the name of Ryan Wilson represented England and Salford in those games, and he would in the years to come play again at Old Trafford on a more regular basis, in front of many more spectators, under the surname of Giggs.

A 1-0 victory against Wimbledon on May 2nd 1989 produced Old Trafford's smallest attendance for a United fixture since May 9th 1966 - 23,368. This was only slightly better than the previous number of 23,069, when United defeated Aston Villa 6-1.

In the wake of the Hillsborough Disaster, United unveiled ambitious new plans for an £8 million re-development of the Stretford End. Early suggestions were to build a design similar to that at the Scoreboard End, with executive boxes at the rear and seating and a standing paddock in front. Although in the red at the bank, Chairman Martin Edwards felt that this was the way ahead.

Prior to the start of season 1989-90, the club decided to reduce the ground capacity by 5,646 as a safety measure. The new capacity would now be 50,837, made up as follows: Stretford End 7,168, United Road Paddock 6,292 (both members only), Old Trafford Paddock 1,520, Stretford Paddock 6,357, Scoreboard Paddock 3,742 (visitors section). The remainder consisted the seating sections.

Over the years, Old Trafford has not produced much in the way of pre-match entertainment, having to drift back to the fifties for anything on a regular basis, this coming from the Beswick Prize Band. However, such pre-match entertainment will never be the same again following the events that proceeded the United - Arsenal opening day fixture on Saturday August 19th 1989. Both sets of supporters stood open mouthed as a figure in a United track suit top and shorts emerged from the tunnel and proceeded to juggle a football towards the Stretford End goal before smashing the ball into the back of the net and saluting the crowd. The sun-drenched 47,245 spectators had never witnessed anything like it, and the name of Michael Knighton was soon to be on everyones lips. Knighton's proposed takeover of the club eventually fell through amid acres of newsprint and speculation, which included plans for a 160 bed hotel adjoining the Stretford End.

The Hillsborough disaster had repercussions throughout football, with every club having to deal with ground alterations and developments in a different manner. United being no exception, following a visit from the Greater Manchester Fire and Civil Defence Authorities, after fans disappointed with United's performance against Norwich City on August 30th tried to leave earlier then normal and found themselves locked in. Apparently, the gates were normally opened midway through the second half, but on this occasion they had been missed and it took some time to find the keys. United were asked to unlock all the gates or face the prospects of matches being postponed. The local authorities hoped that the club might be prepared to consider installing hitech electronic gates, at a cost of around £400,000. The club acted quickly and it was agreed to have each exit gate individually supervised throughout each fixture, with the gates being unlocked shortly after kick-off.

A hostile shareholders meeting in early December, disrupted by a bomb scare and much heckling (directed at the top table), brought cries for Chairman Martin Edwards to sell his 57% holding in the club. Surprisingly it was something that he admitted he would consider. A consortium, made up of United directors Amer Midani, Nigel Burrows and Michael Edelson soon became firm favourites to gain control of the troubled club, but as deadlock loomed between the two parties, a group of property developers began to show their interest. They were, however, not interested in the club as the footballing concern, but had an eye for the ground and the surrounding area and also owned by United, with the nearby Salford Docks and Trafford Park already earmarked for re-development, the potential of the Old Trafford site was obvious. The prospect of buying the ground and leasing it back to the club just did not bear thinking about.

Speculation raged for some time over the future of the club, but at the end of the day, the pressure which had been on manager Alex Ferguson as well as Chairman Martin Edwards waned considerably, and the running of the club returned to a form of normality as results and performances improved.

In mid-March, with the Wembley bandwagon gathering momentum, supporters were taken aback with the announcement of plans for the new Manchester 'super stadium' at a cost of around £200 million. With the City hoping to stage the 1996 Olympic Games, such a stadium would be a major requirement, and a site at Barton Cross was seen as ideal for the 80,000 all-seated venue. What upset supporters so much was the suggestion that the new stadium would be shared by both City and United, with their present homes being vacated. Was this something for the future?

Meanwhile, at Old Trafford the fencing surrounding the pitch was reduced in height to 2.1m following one of the 43 recommendations in the Lord Justice Taylor's Hillsborough report. This was no easy job, as the specialist cutting gear brought in to do the job failed to cut through the extremely tough fencing, and fire crews watched in amazement. New electronically controlled exit gates, costing around £140,000, were also installed, which would be of help with the movement of supporters in any emergency.

As the winter gloom around Old Trafford made way for the spring sunshine, the twin towers of Wembley appeared on the horizon and although it took a replay, the F.A. Cup was won at the expense of a spirited Crystal Palace, bringing relief to almost everyone connected with the club.

The manager now had a close season break to assess the playing squad for the European campaign ahead, while the directors announced their plans for further re-developing of the stadium. With the Lord Justice Taylor's Report being endorsed by the government, all First and Second Division stadiums were required to be all-seated. This meant that the Stretford End, the main standing area with a capacity of 7,168, would soon become a mere memory to generations of United supporters.

While some clubs' would be quite content just to install wooden bench seating to the existing terracing, United decided to continue as had been originally intended, way back in 1965, and continue the cantilever roof right round the ground, completely re-developing that end of the ground. Due to the huge cost involved, and there being no immediate rush into this major undertaking, the close season of 1990 saw only a little step along the way to making the ground all-seated, with the United Road Paddock being converted to accommodate 6,292 sitting spectators.

The famous Stretford End, in the late 1980's...
.... but soon to change beyond all recognition.

United's membership scheme still experienced difficulties, with the non-arrival of membership cards at the start of the season resulting in around 700 supporters being locked out of the opening fixture against Coventry City on August 25th. Temporary memberships were issued, but failed to ease the problem, with many clearly unhappy at having paid £7 for their membership and missing the opening match of the season.

Following the dramatic Lee Martin winner in the F.A. Cup Final replay against Crystal Palace at Wembley, United looked forward to competing in European football again, in the Cup-Winners Cup, as the ban on English clubs' in all European competitions was now lifted. The first European fixture at Old Trafford since Videoton's visit in 1984-85 brought another unknown Hungarian side to Manchester - Pecsi Munkas - and for some supporters in the newly named North Stand Lower

it was watched from behind higher than normal fences, as UEFA regulations forced United to put the new safety fence at full height for all European fixtures. This did little to spoil the supporters enjoyment as United celebrated their return to Europe with a 2-0 victory. The attendance, however, was a disappointing 28,411, the lowest to attend a European match, a record which stretched to some 38 home ties.

Live screening by ITV certainly affected the numbers, which in normal circumstances would have brought a passionate full house to Old Trafford as had similar nights in the past. A night, thought by many as a typical Manchester autumn evening of driving rain and blustery winds, did not help much either in persuading many to leave their armchairs, but the £300,000 offered by ITV for the live showing of both legs was enough for United. All eyes were firmly upon United's travelling support in the return leg of the Cup-tie in Hungary, but thankfully for both club and country those who made the long journey behaved impeccably, receiving praise from many sources.

Seventeen days later, on October 20th, the type of behaviour not wanting to be seen on any European trip was witnessed by 47,232 spectators at Old Trafford plus thousands more on Match of the Day and news programmes later that evening (as well as those watching the game live on TV in 64 countries abroad), when United and Arsenal players became involved in a massive 21 man confrontation in front of the main stand. In the 60th minute of the match, with Arsenal leading 1-0, a touchline clash between Limpar and Irwin prompted the involvement of McClair and Winterburn, as referee Keith Hackett moved in to quell their anger.

Within a minute, a further challenge by Limpar and Winterburn on Irwin brought not only McClair once again into the fray but also every other player on the pitch, with the exception of Seaman the Arsenal 'keeper. Despite the attempted intervention of both benches, the squabble continued for some two minutes before calm was restored. Surprisingly, the only action taken by the referee was to book Limpar and Winterburn! The resulting F.A. commission proved costly to both clubs' with a £50,000 fine and the loss of two points to Arsenal and a similar fine but with only one point deducted from United.

With Christmas looming on the horizon, United would soon raise the money to pay their fine through the takings from the revamped Souvenir Shop, with around 1000 supporters per hour passing through the doors on a matchday keeping the staff on their toes. The shop, a far cry from the small wooden hut which first sold a handful of United Souvenirs in the mid-sixties, now contained a vast catalogue of goods and catered for every taste and pocket, pushing United to the forefront of commercialisation.

Although money seemed to be no problem for the club they always welcomed the lump sums available in the forms of grants for ground improvements. In early February, the Football Trust awarded the club £132,000 to help pay for the installation of seats in the North Stand Lower.

It was hoped the sum of around £2 million would follow at a later date when the Stretford End would be turned into an all-seated section, at a cost of around £13 million. An additional £1 million was also paid out in the summer of 1991 to install seating in front of stands B and C and replacing existing seating in F,G,H and J. The latter would be done in red and white making the word Manchester, with the United on the seats in the lower section.

The European campaign, which had begun back in September, ended in triumph against Spanish giants Barcelona in Rotterdam. This third Cup Final appearance in a year, following the Rumbelow's Cup defeat against Sheffield Wednesday a few weeks previously and the F.A. Cup victory the previous May, helped towards the announcement of a £5.5 million profit and played a major part in the decision to go public on the Stock Exchange. Shares would be sold at £3.85 valuing the club at £47 million.

The playing surface was surprisingly still causing problems, but although United brought the curtain down on a memorable season on May 8th with the visit of Tottenham Hotspur, some of the necessary work could not be carried out for almost three weeks due to the England Challenge Cup match between Argentina and USSR, and after numerous attempts over the years, a rock concert, starring football loving superstar Rod Stewart backed by Status Quo and Joe Coker. Earlier in the month United had also hosted the Rugby Premiership Finals. A crowd of 39,900 attended the concert on Friday the 7th of June to listen to the gravel voiced singer and the support acts churn out their hits from the stage built in front of the Stretford End. Entrance on the night was through the turnstiles on the Warwick Road End of the ground with the haloed turf accommodating much of the crowd.

Pre-season friendlies are normally rather meaningless affairs and used merely as workouts for the months ahead. Included in the fixtures arranged for the summer of 1991, however, was one that meant much more to anyone with an interest in United - a testimonial match for Sir Matt Busby, against the Republic of Ireland on August 11th.

A pre-match curtain raiser saw some of the players who enabled Sir Matt to achieve his dream of lifting the European Cup, take on a team of former Manchester City players. A little thinner on top and broader around the waist, but the 33,40 crowd still warmed to the talents of Kidd, Sadler, Crerand, Charlton and the still enigmatic George Best, before Sir Matt appeared on the touchline to a tremendous ovation and presentation to the crowd and both teams. Sadly United could not produce a victory for the United President, being held to a 1-1 draw by a strong Republic team.

Back in the halcyon days of messrs Best and co., Old Trafford could safely accommodate some 60,000 odd spectators, but in recent times the capacity has shrunk to nearer 40,000, with 43,000 being the limit when the ground became all seated with the reconstruction of the Stretford End. Fans began to voice their opinions at the government enforced changes and numerous suggestions were made in an attempt to maintain the capacity at a level on par with the support enjoyed by the club. Among those suggestions was lowering the level of the pitch to enable more seating to be installed, but this was impractical as UEFA had a ruling limiting how close spectators could be to the playing area. Raising the roof round the stadium and adding extra tiers and a balcony, along with the building of a double decker stand at the Stretford End were also suggested, but discarded for numerous reasons.

On November 16th, the European Super Cup was contested at Old Trafford between United - holders of the European Cup Winners Cup - and a familiar name from the past, Red Star Belgrade, holders of the European Cup. Normally played on a home and away basis, this season saw the tie played as a one off due to the civil war in Yugoslavia making a second leg impossible. United, however, agreed to split the gate receipts with Red Star after suggestions were made by UEFA to play the match in Bari, Italy, and selling the match to television. The attendance attracted in the neutral country would be minimal and so Old Trafford hosted its first Super Cup match. As it was, a share of the gate money and further revenue from Sportscast who were to show the game live in pubs and clubs across the north west and to homes in Europe, made it more profitable.

A 7.15 kick off to accommodate the television coverage was slightly earlier than normal for the United supporters and a chilly November evening saw only 22,110 turn up (an attendance that was more than 11,000 down on the Rumbellow's Cup-tie against Cambridge the previous month). The small band of visiting supporters helped create something of an atmosphere in keeping with the fixture, with smoke bombs exploding into the night air as the game got off to a vibrant start. After only two minutes, Belodedic handled Martin's cross inside the area, but the usually dependable Steve Bruce saw his spot kick saved by Milojevic.

The European Cup holders treated the Manchester crowd to some entertaining football, but failed to turn the chances into goals. A fine save from Schmeicel, followed by a goal line clearance from Blackmore kept Panceu out, while at the other end the Yugoslav 'keeper did not give his defence the greatest of confidence with some of his actions. Savicevic should have given the visitors the lead early in the second half with a 15 yard run followed by a shot which went narrowly wide.

In the 67th minute, against the run of play, the deadlock was finally broken. A 20 yard drive from Webb, who had dispossessed Savicevic, hit an upright and Brian McClair was on hand to tap the ball home from close range. United managed to keep the visitors at bay for the remainder of the match and it was Steve Bruce and his shirted team-mates who took the applause on the lap of honour.

In the meantime, the stadium was in the list of venues confirmed by the F.A. as one of those that would be used if their bid to host the 1996 European Championships was successful. Having been one of the host grounds for the World Cup ties thirty years earlier, it was an obvious choice.

Chairman Martin Edwards, well aware of the supporters discontent over the proposed reduction in capacity the following season, tried to pour water on the flames by announcing that if there was a continual increase in attendances then the board would consider increasing the ground capacity at a later stage. There had been talk of a double-decker stand, but restricted viewing and costs made such developments impractical.

Fan fury ignited again following an announcement that due to the reduced capacity for season 1992-93, admission prices would increase by 50%. Trying to quell the growing revolt, it was suggested that away fans could be excluded to help accommodate more United supporters.

One worry the supporters need not have was on the safety aspect of the ground. Along with the club doctor and 40 St. John's Ambulance staff, there were also 7 other doctors and 14 nurses situated at various points around the stadium in case of any emergency. Perhaps psychiatrists and psychologists would also have been worth giving facilities to, if reports in the American 'National Enquirer' newspaper were anything to go by. In November, it was reported that, *"at a recent Manchester United home fixture, 47,000 fans were scared out of their wits and screamed in terror, when a UFO hovered above them. Within seconds, they were shrieking in panic and pointing to the sky. Players were running in a frantic daze, aware that they were being watched by aliens"* (!) A photographer had supplied the newspaper with four photographs and a supporter gave an eye witness account, but surprisingly (?) nothing appeared in the British press. However, a fixture against Wimbledon could I suppose produce anything!

Around the same time as the 'UFO visit',the pitch was coming in for much criticism from both United and visiting teams and was considered to be *"a nightmare to play on"*. It was in better condition than the previous season, but was still some way from being ideal following the laying of undersoil heading.

Despite the fans reservations regarding ticket pricing and reduction of ground capacity, they could always be guaranteed to get behind the team and produce the magical Old Trafford atmosphere. The evening of March 11th brought Second Division Middlesbrough to Manchester for the 2nd leg of the Rumbellow's Cup Semi-Final, with the teams having played a goalless first leg up in the North East. The match produced one of those memorable Old Trafford occasions, despite the rain and driving wind, with the Second Division side giving a good account of themselves and almost producing something of a shock.

In the opening minutes, they almost took a surprise lead, when Wilkinson moved in ahead of Steve Bruce to send Slavin's cross narrowly over. Irwin came equally close at the opposite end, firing a fisted clearance by Pears, following Webb's free kick, just wide. The saturated surface tested both sets of players and clear-cut chances were few, but a flowing move combining Ince, Robson, Giggs and McClair produced the first breakthrough for United, when Webb supplied the final pass for Sharpe to place an angled shot beyond the reach of former United 'keeper Pears, after 30 minutes.

Five minutes into the second half, the visitors were level as Slaven left-footed a low cross into the United net. As the Middlesbrough fans voiced their encouragement, United almost regained the lead, with Irwin again coming close, while Schmeichel had to save at Wilkinson's feet as play went from end to end. Pallister cleared off the line from Hendrie and with the visitors pressing Falconer just failed to meet a Slavin cross. Neither side could provide the necessary breakthrough and the match drifted into extra-time, which, considering the conditions, was going to be a test for both teams.

A minute into the second period of extra time, a cross from Webb was headed into the path of Giggs by Bryan Robson and the young Welshman volleyed home. There was now no coming back for 'Boro. as United held onto their lead to reach the Final, where a 1-0 victory over Nottingham Forest saw the League Cup displayed in the Old Trafford trophy cabinet for the first time.

In the League campaign, United maintained a strong challenge up until the final few games of the season, only to see their Yorkshire rivals Leeds move in and snatch the trophy from their grasp. With the tears of despair still being wiped away, the club revealed plans for the £12m new look Stretford End, a complex which would take Old Trafford into the next century and maintain its position as the best ground in the country.

The complete end of the ground would be redeveloped ,and when completed would house 10,500 spectators with the inclusion of a new family section, 46 executive boxes, lounges and restaurants. For the VIP supporter, 864 seats in the centre of the stand were earmarked for executive suite members, with lifts to ferry them to and from the three new lounge areas below. The Family Stand was to be moved into one corner of the Stretford End, with 4,000 seats given over to this section and thereby doubling the seating capacity. A purpose-built TV studio would also be incorporated into the construction, to the rear of which would be the new family area.

1992: The Stretford End. (Top) After demolition, with work in progress, and (Below) the finished Stand.

Despite the money that the club was putting into the rebuilding and the up-dating of the stadium with an eye for the future, many supporters found cause to complain as regards to the new plans, but Chairman Martin Edwards said he was proud of what the club had achieved and he felt that United had the finest stadium in the country. And so, on Saturday May 2nd 1992, the League curtain came down on the Stretford End, with the visit of Tottenham Hotspur. Synonymous with the name of Manchester United, it had for years been the vocal section of the stadium, with many of those seated in the stands and in the comfort of the private boxes who had watched United many years before from their favourite spot on the concrete terracing. Everyone who had stood on this - sometimes considered notorious - section of the ground had a favourite memory and many of those were recalled in the pages of the 'United Review' for the Tottenham match.

Following the F.A. Youth Cup Final victory over Crystal Palace on May 5th, the bulldozers moved in and by early June, the demolition firm of Connell and Finnigan of Dukinfield had reduced the entire end to little more than a few heaps of soil and the odd pile of rubble. Many supporters made a point of visiting the ground to obtain a brick or two of the old walls as a reminder of the part of the ground that was for many the heart of Manchester United. Unfortunately, during the demolition work, one workman died in a 50 feet fall from the roof.

Work was also carried out on the other sections of the stadium during the summer, with part of the main stand roof being stripped off and replaced by translucent sheets which would allow the sunshine to filter through and improve the growing of the grass. Many had seen the condition of the pitch as an additional handicap in the title chase of the previous season, and anything was worth considering if it helped improve the surface. Another attempt to save the wear and tear of the pitch was to switch reserve team fixture for the forthcoming 1992-93 season to Gigg Lane, Bury. Additionally, in the main stand at the rear of section A, a police control room had been constructed. Containing a bank of monitors and other electronic equipment, it would enable the stadium safety officer and the police to keep a closer watch on the situation both inside and outside the stadium.

Around £275,000 was spent on a new public address system, which involved some 10 miles of cable, 500 loudspeakers and an amplifier weighing one ton. The benefit would be heard by spectators in all sections of the ground. A new electronic scoreboard was installed, and considering 'Sharps' involvement with the club it was not before time. Would there be an improvement many wondered?

One new development which would not be seen or be of any benefit to the supporter, was a press conference centre underneath the main stand. This auditorium, which would feature in the ground tours, and was to contain comfortable seating on a sloping floor like a cinema with a raised platform at one end. This would be used for the after match press conference and on other occasions, such as player signings when there was a large media turn out.

Two areas which had always been situated below the main stand were scheduled to move with the completion of the new Stretford End stand - the players lounge and the dressing rooms. The former could be considered rather plain and little different from a lounge bar in a hotel, although one distinctive feature was a large honours board containing the names of all the players who had represented the club at international level in the post war years. On the other hand, the dressing rooms, although not identical, would be of an impressively high standard and would be able to accommodate 22 players and managerial team comfortably. To one side were toilets, spa pool - but in the 'home' area only - baths and showers, while on the other (but not for the visitors) was a small warm up room. Televisions were also included.

From the dressing rooms, the players would approach the pitch down a wide tunnel with extending covering for their protection from the crowd. One interesting feature would be the hydraulic lifting equipment at the mouth of the tunnel which would enable the roof to be raised 25 feet in order to allow large screens or other equipment to be moved onto the pitch for closed circuit TV showing or other events. At the opposite end of the ground, a further 60 seats had been installed in the visiting supporters section in L stand, while stand C was enlarged with a further 200 seats.

Outside the stadium, close season work was also evident. Toilets had been constructed outside the museum entrance, while the Souvenir Shop was now around 3,000 square feet in size, after taking over the Development Association premises next door, with the latter moving to a new building across the railway bridge on Warwick Road. The cost of all these additions and alterations? A mere £1m! October 1992 brought supporters an opportunity to take the new 1½ hour tour of the stadium. For £4.95 adults and £2.95 juniors and OAP's, visitors could see for themselves all the alterations to the ground as well as the museum and trophy room.

Hundreds of players had worn the famous red shirt of United since Old Trafford became the club home and many have played their first senior game on the hallowed turf, while others have run out to be greeted by the fans for the first time after joining United from another club.

Johnny Carey, captain of the 1948 F.A. Cup winning side made his first United appearance against Southampton on September 25th 1937. The legendary Duncan Edwards on April 4th 1953 against Cardiff City. Bobby Charlton against Charlton Athletic on October 6th 1956, while his team-mate George Best made his debut against West Bromwich Albion on September 14th 1963. However, on December 6th 1992, the visit of Manchester City for the 117th derby match saw another debutant added to the long illustrious list.

His signing, just over a week earlier, had caused a few eyebrows to be raised and had come as much as a shock and a surprise to the Old Trafford faithful. But, in the years ahead he was going to claim just as many headlines, front and back pages, as George Best, and become one of the United all-time greats. His name of course was Eric Cantona. Sadly, the Frenchman could not begin his career with a goal after coming on as substitute after the interval for the injured Ryan Giggs. Goals from Paul Ince and Mark Hughes gave United a 2-1 victory, but there was plenty of time for the new signing to etch his name in the history books.

Work on the new Stretford End stand continued to schedule and by the end of 1992 the lower section was available to supporters, although there was no protection, other than plastic macs, when it rained. In mid-January, a workman was unfortunately crushed by a ton of concrete in a horrific accident. A concrete girder was being off-loaded and fell, crushing the workman who was immediately rushed to hospital. Unfortunately, nine months later he died.

Friday February 12th saw a significant change take place a short pass from the Old Trafford turnstiles, when Trafford Borough Council officials changed the name of Warwick Road North - which ran from Trafford Park Road past the ground to Chester Road - to 'Sir Matt Busby Way'. A brief unveiling ceremony of one of the new road side signs took place, with the man himself doing the honours, accompanied by the Mayor of Trafford, Councillor Ray Tully, United Chairman Martin Edwards, and manager Alex Ferguson.

United steadily climbed the Premier League after having found themselves anchored at the foot on August 19th, after two games. By January 9th, it was the top spot they occupied and a position that they continued to hold on to despite Aston Villa's challenge. Could the 26 year old jinx finally be at an end? Things were beginning to hot up, and with a local 'derby' against City at Maine Road on March 20th taking on an extra dimension, the decision was made to show the game live on closed circuit TV at Old Trafford. It had been over fifteen years since the last televised match at the ground, and despite the 11am kick off, a crowd of 10,462 surprised United officials by turning up to watch on the big 25' x 19' screen which had been erected in front of the North Stand.

With six games remaining, Sheffield Wednesday visited Old Trafford on April 10th and as the match moved into the final stages, it looked as if the ghosts of seasons past were about to reappear. Wednesday matched United stride for stride throughout the first half, and midway through the second they stunned the packed stadium into silence when they took the lead through a John Sheridan penalty, awarded by John Hilditch who had begun the game as a linesman but had replaced injured referee Michael Peck only minutes before.

United replaced Paul Parker with Bryan Robson almost immediately in an attempt to rescue something from the game and keep their title hopes alive. The United supporters in the 40,102 crowd became increasingly unsettled as the minutes ticked away and watches were being constantly checked.

Six minutes to go, and attacking the old Stretford End, now a magnificent sight with every seat occupied, United won yet another corner and from Denis Irwin's kick, captain Steve Bruce headed home to level the score and send the crowd ecstatic. So often the scorer of vital goals, the big defender had once again save United from the throes of defeat. A draw would have been acceptable, but the United faithful pumped up the volume in the hope that a further goal might be there, even though the final whistle beckoned.

No one, however, had reckoned on the amount of injury time that was still to be played, and 7 minutes 14 seconds over the 90, with every ball being thumped into the Wednesday penalty area, Gary Pallister flicked the ball over his head into the path of the oncoming Steve Bruce, who once again headed past Woods. The noise was deafening and must have been heard in Piccadilly Gardens as the red contingent within the ground became delirious. Alex Ferguson and his assistant Brian Kidd staged a mini pitch invasion, as usually serene neighbours in the stands embraced in a fever, usually reserved for more intimate moments with members of the opposite sex. Seconds later it was all over, United had turned what at one time had looked like a certain defeat into a vital three points in one of the most memorable games seen at the ground.

On April 21st, with United at Crystal Palace, Old Trafford once again showed the match on closed circuit TV. A staggering 15,009 turned up, which was actually larger than Wimbledon's biggest seasonal gate to that time! Once again, the club was caught out by the number of people who were keen to watch the match on the big screen and additional gates had to be opened. Some people arriving at the ground found the queues along Sir Matt Busby Way and 400 yards down Chester Road just a bit too much, and many decided to about turn and go home. Those who did take the time to queue enjoyed a good evening's entertainment, and admitted afterwards that the atmosphere made it seem like a normal home fixture.

Monday May 3rd produced another of those memorable Old Trafford occasions, with visitors Blackburn Rovers playing a mere bit-part, as the long awaited Championship, now a new trophy for the inaugural Premier League season. The ground forecourt had been the venue of an impromptu party since the previous afternoon, when the title had been decided following the defeat of nearest rivals Aston Villa by Oldham Athletic. Supporters soon began arriving at the ground, champagne corks popped in unison to the car horns of passing motorists, as the United songbook received an airing. At one point even United's Lee Sharpe appeared to join in the celebrations. And so it continued, with the pre-match scenes outside the ground taking on a new level with flags and supporters everywhere, and tickets changing hands at Cup Final prices.

It seemed like a giant conga as the same scenes were repeated inside the stadium and didn't even let up when Blackburn took an 8 minute lead through Gallagher. The sun drenched stadium continued to party. Thirteen minutes later a tremendous Ryan Giggs free kick got things back on the right track, and further goals from Paul Ince and Gary Pallister emphasised the superiority of the Champions. For once, there were no early departures before the final whistle, as no one had any intentions of missing the presentation of the glistening trophy to team and club captains Steve Bruce and Bryan Robson.

Tina Turner's 'Simply The Best' boomed out yet again from the public address system as the players went on their lap of honour, something that many present had never witnessed at the ground before, and all hoped to see again with nothing like the wait since the last triumph.

Success on the pitch also brought spin-offs elsewhere, with the Souvenir shop on the day of the Blackburn match recording record receipts. Although exact figures were not made available, it was believed that around £100,000 was taken over the counter. With the new Premier League trophy as top attraction in the United museum, all sights were set on its retention as season 1993-94 drew near.

The Old Trafford curtain-raiser was the match against old adversaries Benfica, a fixture arranged as part of the 25th anniversary celebrations of winning the European Cup. On the day of the match the stadium had never looked better, with the new Stretford End stand setting it off perfectly, with its red and white seating showing the word Umbro along the lower section and their diamond shape trade mark on the upper.

Some concern was shown regarding the South Stand, as the contractors struggled to complete the £2.5m facelift which included the installation of 600 new seats and the re-alignment of the gangways. Thankfully the club's embarrassment was spared as the unfinished section was not required, with only a disappointing 20,800 turning up for the Benfica match, to watch an uneventful ninety minutes which the visitors won 1-0.

By August 18th, and the opening home League fixture against Sheffield United, United had paid out almost £15m in 15 months. Most of this outlay had gone on the new stand development, with around £5m on the South Stand and other areas. The Sheffield fixture, saw for the first time, the ground fully operational after all the close season work, and a crowd of 41,949 watched a pre-match presentation of the Premier League Championship flag to manager Alex Ferguson and Chairman Martin Edwards. The giant flag would be flown from the pole on top of the North Stand on matchdays.

Prior to the European Cup-tie against Honved on September 29th, Frank Taylor the only surviving journalist from the Munich Air Disaster, unveiled a new Press Memorial Plaque in the press lounge. The original plaque, which had been stolen some years previously, used to be sited above the entrance into the press box, but the replacement plaque had been removed during the summer renovations and it was decided to find a new place for it.

Over the years, many hardened professionals have both angered and inspired the Old Trafford crowds. Men like Frank Barson, Nobby Stiles, Mark Hughes, Bryan Robson and Roy Keane in the red of United, along with opponents such as Norman Hunter, Dave Mackay and Vinnie Jones, but two real hard men faced each other on the Old Trafford pitch on the evening of Saturday October 9th, when Nigel Benn faced Chris Eubank for the World Super-Middleweight Boxing Championship of the World. The famous hallowed turf was completely covered over, with the ring erected in the centre, for what had become known as 'Judgement Day', and over 40,000 fight fans turned up for the confrontation between the two deadly rivals. This broke the post-war gate record set when Henry Cooper took on Cassius Clay at Highbury in 1964. After 12 rather uneventful rounds, which must have disappointed the like of Sir Matt Busby and the other spectators, the judges declared the outcome a draw.

Following the fight, however, there were numerous complaints. Many of the ringside spectators, who had paid £250 to watch the fight were upset because their area had been infiltrated by others, while another complaint arose from there only being 5 instead of 7 bouts. After the event, many were left stranded at the ground when the expected late night transport failed to turn up. Perhaps a football ground is, after all, only for football!

Restricted from fielding the team which brought the title to the club by UEFA regulations over the number of non-English players that a club could field, United's European dreams were shattered by the relatively unknown Turkish side Galatasaray. A 0-0 draw in Turkey was enough to take the home side through on the away goals ruling, as they had stunned the Old Trafford crowd by scoring three in a dramatic first leg. With only eight minutes remaining in that first game, it looked as if United's proud home record of never having lost a European tie at home was about to be brought to an end. In hope and desperation, more than anything else, Roy Keane lofted a high ball towards the visitors goal, where Eric Cantona managed to evade his marker to stab the ball home.

The game produced many talking points, but perhaps the main one that concerned the club (other than the result) were the two incidents involving visiting supporters. In one, Kurdish protesters managed to evade the touchline security and got onto the pitch brandishing a burning Turkish flag. As police and stewards moved towards the trespassers, United's goalkeeper Peter

Schmeichel sprinted from his goal and unceremoniously began to remove one of them from the pitch, much to the concern of the Turkish players and the delight of the home support. A second incident involved the throwing of a full soft drinks can onto the pitch which narrowly missed a Turkish player. Fortunately there were no severe repercussions for United.

On the evening of Thursday January 20th, the football world was stunned by the announcement that Sir Matt Busby had died. The man, who more than any other was responsible for the worldwide adoration of the club and the magnificent stadium it called home, would no more be seen on a matchday, walking slowly across the forecourt with members of his family to the acknowledgement of the supporters, to watch his beloved team.

For many, Sir Matt was Manchester United, and vice versa, and as the news broke across the city, supporters began to arrive at the ground, simply to pay their respects to the great man. Some laid bunches of flowers against the wall of the stadium, underneath the Munich memorial, while others left their scarves. The following day saw countless others make the same pilgrimage and the forecourt was soon a carpet of flowers, scarves and memorabilia. Inside the museum was a book of remembrance for the fans to sign, and there was also a small area given over to a large photograph of Sir Matt along with numerous flowers and wreaths.

Saturday, the 22nd, was matchday, and it had been obvious over the last couple of days that it would be no ordinary one. From early morning, there are always people scattered around the ground, but today there were more than usual. Television crews mingled with the increasing numbers on the forecourt as the carpet of scarves etc. took on new dimensions. As 3pm approached, those with match tickets were already inside, determined for once not to be late, while outside there were still around an estimated 15,000, content at simply just being there on the day. Manchester United paid its last respects to its President.

As an announcement from the public address system asked the crowd to stand. The first strains of a piper could be heard from the mouth of the

players tunnel in the corner of the Stretford End. The haunting melody of 'A Scottish Soldier' grew louder as the lone piper lead the players of United and Everton onto the pitch, followed by officials of both clubs. There were lumps in many throats and numerous tears were unashamedly shed. With the piper now silent, and both teams lined up in the centre of the pitch, an eerie silence fell on the ground. Following the respected silence, the United supporters in the 44,750 crowd applauded the Everton followers for their show of respect.

In the ninety minutes of football, which Sir Matt would have enjoyed, United played some vintage stuff, but could only win by a solitary Ryan Giggs goal. The young Welshman displayed his wide array of skills and Cantona displayed his usual panache in midfield, but the day would always be remembered for only one reason.

A week after his death, on Thursday January 27th, came Sir Matt's funeral at Our Lady and St. Johns Church in Chorlton-cum-Hardy. Following a moving service, attended by some 90 former players, the funeral procession made its way towards the lasting memorial to Sir Matt - Old Trafford. Sir Matt Busby Way, and beyond, was lined with over 5,000 supporters caring nothing for the rain which fell, and with the Munich clock showing 12.06, the hearse, followed by 14 cars and 3 coaches came to a halt outside the ground.

For two silent tear-jerking minutes, the crowd bowed heads, remembered 'the Boss', and the three fabulous sides that he created, before a horn blew and the hearse pulled away from the ground towards Southern Cemetery. Inside, the stadium stood empty and one seat, No.B122 in Row 25 would remain so as a mark of respect.

With Old Trafford already chosen as one of the venues for the Euro '96 competition, the stadium was also put forward as the new home for England international games as a row between Wembley and the F.A. simmered. Although with a smaller capacity than the national stadium - 45,000 opposed to 75,000 - United argued that at least everyone at Old Trafford could see, and the overall facilities were better. Such a move would of course be well received in the north if it ever came to pass, but time will only tell if future internationals would be played away from Wembley.

Over the years, many clubs have found it difficult to obtain a result against United at home, but perhaps the best record in recent times is held by Chelsea, with the fixture between the two on March 5th proving the point, with the Londoners bringing the treble chasing United side to a temporary halt. Although not a result, or a performance for the record books, it was still a notable day in the life of the stadium.

Prior to the match, a record number of people - 1,148 - paid to enjoy the memorabilia in the United museum prior to the match. Some lower division clubs have to survive on similar numbers passing through their turnstiles. The previous museum record had been 980. On the same day, Manchester United Radio was launched from Old Trafford, providing news and views and match commentary to those living within a five mile radius of the ground. Broadcasting on 1413 AM, the station would transmit for eight hours on match days, beginning at 10.30am, from a custom built studio at the ground. It would be linked to the ground PA system, with the match commentary being transmitted to blind supporters within the ground. Sponsored by greetings card company 'Birthdays', advertising would also help contribute to the running costs. The club itself paid out more than £40,000 to equip the studio.

Music of a different kind echoed around the stadium on Sunday April 24th when a memorial service for Sir Matt Busby was held at the ground. All the flags flew at half mast, as the 10,000 crowd assembled along with past and present United players, show business stars, and members of Sir Matt's family. The moving, hour long service combined singing with spoken tributes from famous names of the past, such as Harry Gregg, Bobby Charlton, Charlie Mitten and Kenneth Wolstenholme. Denis Law and community signing leader Vince Millar sung one of Sir Matt's favourite songs, 'I Belong to Glasgow', while the tears flowed openly as the strains of 'Abide With Me', followed by the Old Trafford anthem 'Walking Down the Warwick Road' drifted into the afternoon air.

The spirit of Sir Matt will always remain at the ground and his memory seemed to inspire the team as the final weeks of the season approached. With the games left to play slowly decreasing, United's retention of the Championship looked highly probable, and as Blackburn Rovers stuttered at Coventry, everyone with Old Trafford connections began to celebrate. The F.A. Cup had also been contested determinedly, and on May 14th the Red Army headed for Wembley, where Chelsea provided little in the way of opposition as United joined the elite list of double winners.

On the eve of the penultimate match of the season, against Southampton at Old Trafford, with the club scaling unforseen heights, the Manchester Evening News carried an article on United's plans for increasing the ground capacity to 64,000 by building a second tier onto one of the stands, a development which would eventually continue around the ground. Each stage would depend on the money available as well as the demand for more seating from the increasing interest from supporters. The club, however, said that there would be no statement regarding such a development until plans had been finalised, and a decision made as to whereabouts it would begin. Once the ground had been completely seated then an announcement would be made.

So, the visit of Coventry City on the 8th May had seen another day of celebrations around the ground, with the presentation of the Championship trophy. Perhaps not on the same scale as the previous years, but it was still an enjoyable and eventful afternoon as it marked the final competitive appearance in the red shirt of club captain Bryan Robson, with many present casting their minds back to his signing on the pitch over a decade earlier. But as one United name made his farewell appearance, another was making his first, as the club unveiled its new mascot - Fred the Red.

The last official club mascot had been Mr. Jack Irons, whose red and white bedecked figure was a familiar sight in the pre-war years. Hopefully he would be better behaved than the mascot associated with the club during the time at Bank Street, who was a goat named Billy. Apparently, he was owned by one of the players of that period and after each home match it would follow the supporters to a nearby public house and drink all the beer bought him until he collapsed on the floor!

With United fans still on the crest of a wave following the double success, they received something of a jolt when stories began to surface involving neighbours City, who were considering renting Old Trafford while building work was carried out on the Kippax Street section of their Maine Road ground. City chairman Francis Lee later shrugged off the idea as a tongue in the cheek remark, and stated that there was little chance of the war time groundshare being reversed.

Interest in the club seemed to be at an all time high, with official membership figures approaching 103,000. Stadium tours and museum visitors (which had reached 100,000 in the first six months of the year) were also on the up. The Super Store also had a constant ringing of tills, making the name 'Gold Trafford' seem much more appropriate. Sell-outs and over demand for tickets were therefore regular occurrences and Sunday September 25th saw yet another 40,000 full house at the ground with a further 10,000 ticket applicants having been unsuccessful in their bid to be in attendance.

A look at the United fixture list for 1994-95, however, would leave many people thinking that a mistake had been made, but on that particular afternoon, the red shirts were not in sight, as the stadium had been taken over by the BBC to record their familiar Sunday programme - 'Songs of Praise'. Worshippers flocked to the ground from all over the country and made just as colourful a scene as any matchday, with numerous banners being waved around the ground as the air was filled with singing and music the recorded programme. What next for the stadium?

Always alert to any breach of safety regulations, United officials banned a huge 130' x 60' red, black and white flag from the ground in early October. Owned by supporter Mike Edroff, the flag was unfurled and passed over the heads of the supporters as it made its way around the ground, but the fear of it igniting forced the club to ban it. However, they did add that if Mike could obtain a safety certificate for it they would allow it back into the ground.

The suggestion of a second tier around the ground which had been made towards the end of the previous season took on a new meaning early in October, when a David Meek 'exclusive' in the Manchester Evening News revealed that the club planned to 'Reach for the Sky', with a triple decker stand to take the place of the existing cantilever one which ran along United Road, which was built for the 1966 World Cup. A feasibility study had been commissioned, and Sir Roland Smith, chairman of the main board, admitted that, *"there were quite a number of options to consider"*.

Much would depend on the continued success on the playing side and also the availability of that land owned by Trafford Park Estates adjacent to the United Road, which would be required if such a development was to take place.

With Manchester looking to build a new stadium in order to host major sports events such as the Olympic Games - or perhaps more realistically the Commonwealth Games - there was also a possibility of moving away from Old Trafford altogether, to a brand new home. Supporters, however, were very much against such a move ever being considered.

Football memorabilia today is big business, with collectors paying hundreds of pound for programmes, autographs and other items relating to the club and the players who have pulled on the famous red jersey over the years. At a tribute dinner to Bryan Robson, perhaps one of the most unusual items to become available appeared during a charity auction held as part of the evening. Hidden behind a curtain was a huge old hoarding from the ground, which dated back to the early seventies, and depicted a diagram of the stadium.

United players at the dinner, as well as supporters, were speechless as the curtain was drawn back to reveal the sign, which had mysteriously disappeared during renovations some years previously and had not been seen since. It had came into the possession of a United supporter who thought that it would be ideal to use as a means for raising money for charity, and subsequently it appeared at the auction where it was bought by a company boss who intended to give it pride of place in his offices, but refused to admit to the press what he had paid for it.

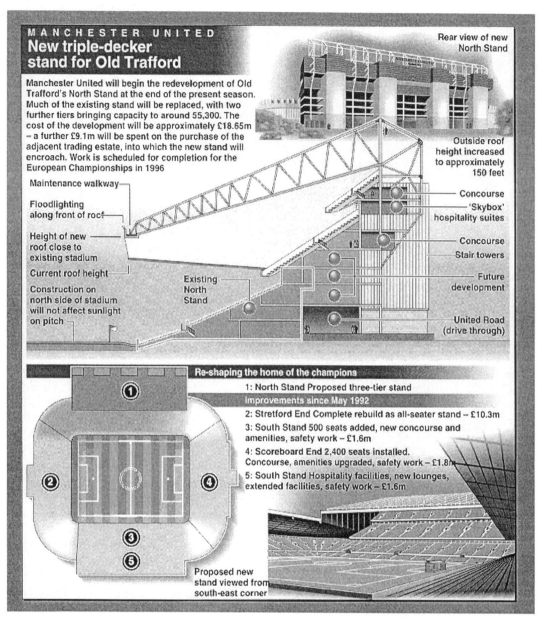

MANCHESTER UNITED
New triple-decker stand for Old Trafford

Rear view of new North Stand

Manchester United will begin the redevelopment of Old Trafford's North Stand at the end of the present season. Much of the existing stand will be replaced, with two further tiers bringing capacity to around 55,300. The cost of the development will be approximately £18.65m – a further £9.1m will be spent on the purchase of the adjacent trading estate, into which the new stand will encroach. Work is scheduled for completion for the European Championships in 1996

Outside roof height increased to approximately 150 feet

Maintenance walkway

Floodlighting along front of roof

Height of new roof close to existing stadium

Current roof height

Construction on north side of stadium will not affect sunlight on pitch

Existing North Stand

Concourse

'Skybox' hospitality suites

Concourse

Stair towers

Future development

United Road (drive through)

Re-shaping the home of the champions

1: North Stand Proposed three-tier stand

Improvements since May 1992

2: Stretford End Complete rebuild as all-seater stand – £10.3m

3: South Stand 500 seats added, new concourse and amenities, safety work – £1.6m

4: Scoreboard End 2,400 seats installed. Concourse, amenities upgraded, safety work – £1.8m

5: South Stand Hospitality facilities, new lounges, extended facilities, safety work – £1.6m

Proposed new stand viewed from south-east corner

The proposed triple-decker Stand, as depicted in 1994
by Management Contractors Hilstone Laurie.

By mid-November, the plans for the new towering second tier to be added onto the North Stand were on show at Trafford Borough Council. The construction, which would dwarf the rest of the stadium would reach almost 160 feet in height, making it around 94 feet higher than the existing stand. In order to build such a structure, United Road would have to be altered, as it would extend some 60 feet outwards.

A new access road would need to be built, and a further 90 full and part-time jobs would be created to service the new construction. Club secretary, Ken Ramsden confirmed that United were in negotiations with Trafford Park Estates to purchase the land required to implement the plans. Two months later, the Trafford Park Development Corporation had approved the plans and the Trafford Council were in agreement towards the triple decker development.

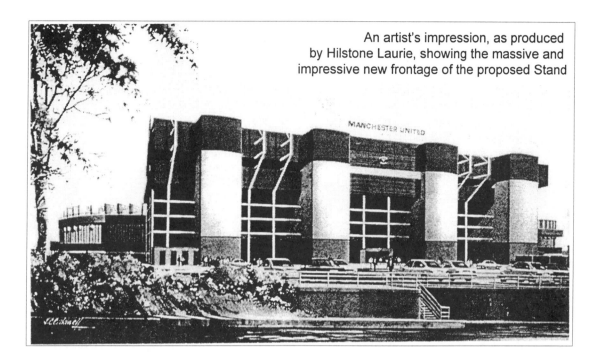

An artist's impression, as produced by Hilstone Laurie, showing the massive and impressive new frontage of the proposed Stand

The plans had not been straightforward for the club as some angry clashes had occurred between rival factions on the council, who felt that local residents were perhaps not being considered as the club was increasing its capacity and bringing more people into the area on match days. With planning permission now secured, funding of the venture was now the main concern.

As the imaginations of the supporters ran riot with thoughts of what the new stand would look like, the stadium - as it then stood - received the seal of approval from the UEFA stadium inspectors who were visiting all the proposed Euro '96 venues. Chairman of the committee, Mr Ernie Walker, gave the ground the supreme accolade of the 'Best in Britain'. *"I know that Wembley is bigger"*, he said, *"but it is not better than Old Trafford"*. Along with fellow committee members, the ground was inspected for security and facilities for the media, along with segregation arrangements.

December 3rd saw Norwich City visit Old Trafford and manager Alex Ferguson had to break away from his normal match day routine to officially open the new United Mega Store, situated behind the Stretford End of the ground, where the illustrious names in the club's past used to play five-a-side as part of their training routine.

At 10.30am, the former goalscoring centre-forward kicked a ball through a paper net to declare the store open, as the queues stretched back towards the spot where the original wooden hut stood which first sold United souvenirs. Crammed with everything from tiny strips for babies, curtains and bedding, to wallpaper and a United Trivial Pursuit game with 4,000 questions, the Mega Store could be considered every parents nightmare. The new store closed at one minute to three, re-opened at half time for those without tickets for the match, and again at full time. As the last supporters drifted home with their carrier bags bulging, the days takings were reported at an astonishing £250,000!

Certain fixtures provide the supporter with ninety minutes to remember and the opportunity to say *"I was there"*, when the game is recalled on various occasions in the future. Such a match occurred at the ground on March 3rd 1995, when Ipswich Town journeyed north from East Anglia to fulfil a Premier League fixture. Most players enjoy their seasonal visit to Old Trafford, but for the Ipswich goalkeeper Craig Forrest it was one to forget as United recorded a 9-0 victory. Forrest, it must be said, did not play badly, it was simply a case of him and his teammates coming up against United on a day when everything clicked together.

The day undoubtedly belonged to Andy Cole, signed from Newcastle United in January for £7m, who claimed 5 goals, (although one could be considered an own goal), the highest number scored by a United player in a League match. United attacked right from the start and had the Ipswich goal under pressure on a few occasions before Keane opened the scoring in the 15th minute. The second followed four minutes later as Cole claimed his first from a Giggs cross.

It wasn't until eight minutes before the interval that the third goal was scored, although the visitors could have pulled one back before. A McClair - Kanchelskis move created an opportunity for Hughes, who was unlucky to see his bicycle kick hit the bar. With the crowd still on their feet, Cole nipped in to score with the rebound. After the interval, the floodgates opened, and three goals in 6 minutes finished the game as a contest. The 'Cole/own goal' made it four in the 53rd minute. Hughes fired home two minutes later to make it five and the same player made it six in the 59th minute with a header. It was now a case of how many, as Ipswich all but gave up. Cole netted the seventh in the 65th minute as McClair's shot was pushed out by Forrest, while a cheeky free kick by Ince, with the Ipswich 'keeper stranded outside his area after conceding the kick, dropped into the unguarded goal. With the Ipswich players and their supporters longing for the final whistle, the scoreboard (thankfully working that afternoon) changed to 9-0 as Cole hit his fifth, to re-write the history books. It was the highest League victory since the 9-0 defeat of Darwen in a Second Division fixture on December 24th 1898.

The imagination of local based supporters could at last ease back to normality, as on Tuesday March 17th the front page of the Manchester Evening News carried a photograph of the scale model of the new super stadium, following Chairman Martin Edwards' announcement that, *"the biggest, most costly and the most ambitious development ever undertaken by Manchester United"*, would go ahead eight days after planning permission had been given.

With the club given the green light, the project team was put together, consisting of construction manager Hilstone Laurie, architect Atherden Fuller, structural engineer Campbell Reith Hill, and mechanical and electrical engineer W E.Hannan. The majority of the team had been together for the Stretford End development, with the architects having been responsible for the original cantilever stand on United Road in 1965.

Tim Laycock, regional director of Hilstone Laurie, revealed that the team's original proposals were to construct a new two tier stand, cantilevered over the top of the existing North Stand, simply to increase the ground capacity, but they were concerned that the 30 year-old building would prove too expensive to re-design to modern standards. With United very much concerned on providing first class amenities for their supporters and improving safety, the team decided to put forward a proposal to demolish the whole stand and replace it with a new steel construction. Even that was not completely straightforward, as thirteen different proposals were considered before the final decision was made.

For those interested in the merest detail, the stand would measure 114m long by 60m wide, rising 45m above the pitch at its highest point. The roof would be constructed in tubular sections, made up into 16 main roof trusses measuring 66m long and tapering in depth from 9.8m to 2m. Some 3,500 tonnes of steel would be used, along with 4,500 tonnes of concrete in the form of 10,000 sq.m of pre-cast seating units which would take 185 wagons to deliver. A total of 14,800 individual pieces of steel were to be incorporated!

The three tiers would be divided into eight seating levels, with 8,000 sq.m earmarked for restaurants and a new museum. Fans in the top tier would sit at a steep 34 degree angle above the horizontal, while the second tier would be a mere 30 degrees. The cost of the development was expected to be around £28m, with some £9.1m of that total going towards the purchase of land along the United Road which would be straddled by the new stand. This was actually almost £3m more than the market value. Seating 25,111, the Old Trafford capacity would rise to 55,300, thus becoming the largest club stadium in the country. This would include 64 private boxes, with increased seating in the lower sections.

Early Summer 1995, and work is well underway on the demolition of the 'old' North Road Stand

The only minus points about the plans was that the next season would see a reduced ground capacity to a mere 33,000, with almost all of those being Season Ticket and League Match Ticket holders, leaving little or no space for the ordinary club member.

The Hilstone Laurie contract would be dictated by five stages, and as each stage was completed it was hoped to be able to release further seating to the supporters, with the entire job scheduled for completion in April 1996.

The home fixture, Vs Arsenal, shortly after the defeat of Ipswich, brought further talking points amongst the supporters, with notification that if they stood during the game then they could face ejection from the ground. Many during the course of the match continued the habits of a lifetime, and stood when the excitement got the better of them and goalscoring opportunities arose. Sadly, they found themselves being escorted from the ground by the stewards who had taken over the responsibility from the police for most aspects of

crowd control inside the stadium. The fans, and many others, were not amused and meetings were held in protest. It was hoped that the United board would try and create special areas in the ground where like minded-supporters could sit (or stand) and encourage the team, like the vocal centred Stretford End of the past.

At the end of what proved to be a disappointing season by United's recent standards - runners up in both the League and F.A. Cup - the bulldozers moved in to demolish the United Road stand or' North Stand' which was now its official name. First the seats were removed from both sections, with a state-of-the-art mechanical digger which punched the concrete to pieces, moving in on June 1st. It took just three weeks to reduce the former 12,500 seater stand to a pile of rubble, and by the fourth week in June the site was completely clear and ready for the piling to begin and the new foundations to be laid. By early August, the lower terracing would be in place and it was planned to admit fans into the first tier by the turn of the year.

Due to the progress made on the site, 2,000 additional seats were made available for the opening home fixture of 1995-96 against West Ham. These seats were in the corner sections beside the open site. Wimbledon's visit in the following fixture saw a further 500 available as work progressed ahead of schedule. Such seats only became available a day or two prior to the game due to the necessity of a site inspection to ensure total safety in either area.

Numerous memorable goals have been scored at Old Trafford since its opening back in February 1910. Players in every position, and the odd goalkeeper, have found the back of the net, but we have to go back to season 1973-74 and an Alex Stepney penalty against Birmingham City to recall one by the latter. Competing in the UEFA Cup, the first round draw paired United with the unfamiliar Rotor Volgograd from Russia, and having obtained a creditable 0-0 draw in the first leg away from home, the return was considered a mere formality.

The 29,724 crowd, like the United team and management, received something of a shock as the visitors earned a 2-2 draw and progressed into the next round on the away goal ruling. Some of the supporters, (those who did not leave early in disgust), did have the satisfaction of witnessing the first goal scored at the ground by a goalkeeper as a result of an outfield move.

With the game, like United's proud European home record, looking lost, (Volgograd had taken a 2-0 lead after 24 minutes, with Paul Scholes pulling one back in the 58th minute), a corner at the Scoreboard End in the shadows of the construction work, saw the awesome figure of Peter Schmeichel amble up field to take a threatening position in the Russian area.

This was not his first foray forward, but it proved to be the most profitable, as the green clad figure of the big Dane rose above the opposition defence to head strongly into the back of the net via a defender. A memorable goal on a disappointing night. The Russians, ecstatic with their perform-ance ,were also impressed by the Old Trafford pitch and managed to obtain eight bags of grass seed and two bags of fertiliser, as used by United groundsman Keith Kent!

October 1st 1995, a day that had been marked in red within countless dairies around Britain and beyond, saw Old Trafford resemble Paris on Bastille Day, as countless French tricolours fluttered in the autumn air. The occasion? The return of Eric Cantona to the United side for the first time since his evening of misadventure at Selhurst Park way back in January. The opponents on the day were arch-rivals Liverpool, but it would not have mattered if it was the likes of Hartlepool, it was an occasion not to be missed and never since the sixties has one man meant so much to the United supporters.

The volatile Frenchman did not disappoint his adoring fans and with only 67 seconds gone, his cross was placed beyond Liverpool 'keeper James, by Nicky Butt, to give United the lead. The tricolours were raise and the anthems sung a little louder. Liverpool did not lie down and went on to take a 2-1 lead, but the day was always going to belong to one man and, significantly, he had the last word. In the 69th minute, Giggs was brought down in the box by Redknapp as he moved through, and without a moment's hesitation, Cantona collected the ball, placed it on the spot and proceeded to send James the wrong way, to level the scores.

A draw in any other match against Liverpool would have been a disappointment , but the 'King' was back and he had scored. Stallholders scattered along Sir Matt Busby Way were just as happy, when a few more T-shirts and flags were sold as the fans streamed out of the stadium at full time.

Due to the reduced capacity, United were allowed to ignore the Premier League dispensation recommending that visiting clubs' had to receive 3,000 seats, thus making the ground for home fans only, which made the atmosphere rather subdued. But as the season progressed and work continued ahead of schedule (and to budget), United sought to alter this and give visiting clubs a limited number of tickets. The lack of atmosphere even prompted the Independent Manchester United Supporters Club to draw up a twenty-plus point plan and forward it to Chairman Martin Edwards in the hope that Old Trafford could be restored to a noisy arena in the future.

November 1994: The construction of the massive new structure is well on target

A couple of the suggestions made were that the entire Stretford End of the ground could be designated an area where fans could stand if they wished, with K stand and East Stand Lower (the old Scoreboard End) also being allowed similar usage. Another point was that singing areas should also be created to help improve the atmosphere.

November 1995 saw part of the stadium take on a sponsor, with Express Cargo Forwarding signing a three year deal with the Museum and Tour Centre. More than 500,000 people had visited the museum since it first opened in 1986.

The visit of Southampton on November 18th saw the crowd capacity break the 39,000 barrier for the first time that season, as an addition 7,000 seats had been installed and a safety inspection saw the site pass without any problems. This was six weeks ahead of schedule. With the North Stand Lower having been available since the end of

September, things were returning to normal. Even away fans were re-admitted, with the Hampshire side receiving 800 tickets for J Stand, although segregation reduced the overall ground capacity by 1,000. The advanced stage of re-building was believed to have earned the club an extra £1m in gate revenue.

A month later came the 'Topping Out' ceremony on the triple decker construction. This was a traditional ceremony which saw Chairman Martin Edwards hammer in a golden bolt and a piece of yew branch was tied to part of the roofing to ward off evil spirits.

The F.A. Cup-tie against Manchester City allowed some supporters the privilege of watching the game from the brand new executive boxes at the back of the North Stand, with around 13,000 fellow reds seated below, thanks once again to the rapid progress being made. The attendance for that cup-tie on February 18th was 42,692.

April still looked the likely date to see the project completed, with at least one game towards the end of the season having spectators in every section. It would certainly all be ready for the European Championships, when United, along with Liverpool would host the north-west section - Group C - comprising Germany, Italy, Russia and the Czech Republic. The feast of football was enriched with the prospects of a quarter-final and a semi-final tie also taking place at Old Trafford.

Having sold three experienced, and popular, players during the summer - Ince, Hughes and Kanchelskis - and begun the League campaign with a 4-1 defeat at Aston Villa, many thought that season 1995-96 would be one of rebuilding in two departments at Old Trafford. However, as the months passed by United maintained steady progress and by early March they had clawed back Newcastle's twelve point advantage with some sterling performances. They were also in the quarter-finals of the F.A. Cup with a home draw against Southampton, a match that would see spectators admitted to the second tier of the new stand for the first time. Despite the previous weeks of rather severe weather, work had continued well up to expectations and it was hoped that the last two home fixtures would see the attendance move close to the 55,000 capacity.

Supporters arriving at the ground for the Southampton tie on a very wet Manchester evening could reach the stadium by a new route, as a pedestrian footbridge had been constructed across the Bridgwater Canal, allowing access from Trafford Park Road. This provided easy entry into the new North Stand for spectators using that side of the ground for parking. The Cup-tie also saw the new floodlights along the stand roof used for the first time, with the three temporary pylons which provided a partly obscured view for some spectators due to their situation in the lower section of the North Stand, being removed following the previous home fixture. The attendance for that Southampton Cup-tie, which saw United move to within one game of their third consecutive Wembley Cup Final appearance, was 45,446, almost 3,000 more than the season's previous best.

On the night of Thursday March 12th, Old Trafford had a rare and unwelcome visit by cat-burglars, who caused £10,000 worth of damage in an attempt to break into Chairman Martin Edwards' office. Having scaled a 50ft wall, they smashed a hole in the stadium roof before crawling through a heating duct to gain entry into the office block. Surprisingly the alarm system did not go off and they managed to obtain entry into the Chairman's second floor office, where they located a safe and proceeded to throw it out from a window, onto the concourse below. Having exited the ground, they failed to remove the safe and disappeared into the night. One would have thought that it was nigh impossible for such an incident to occur.

The 1-0 victory over Arsenal on March 20th saw the first 50,000 plus crowd for seven years, as the Championship challenge was maintained. The 50,028 attendance was then bettered by 129 four days later, when the other North London club, Tottenham, were the visitors.

Sunday March 31st was F.A. Cup Semi-Final day and as United travelled south to Villa Park, the followers of the Birmingham side took the opposite route to Old Trafford to face Liverpool in the other tie. Ticket pricing by the F.A. was criticised, and as a result many seats at both Semi-Final venues were left empty, with the 39,072 at Old Trafford being perhaps the most disappointing. United's 2-1 victory over Chelsea saw them move a step closer to a unique second 'double' in three years, something never before achieved.

Easter, the crunch time of any Championship or relegation battle, saw a Manchester 'derby' at Maine Road. Such was the interest in the game, with City fighting against the drop into the First Division that the match was televised live at Old Trafford. Wednesday April 17th brought Yorkshire rivals Leeds United across the Pennines to Old Trafford and some of the red army had the privilege (?) of obtaining tickets for a birds eye view of the game from the very top tier of the North Stand for the first time. Some ten levels and 55 meters up, a climb of 170 steps would leave even the fittest breathless, and it was certainly not advised to arrive at the ground five minutes prior to the kick-off and hope to be in your seat on time!

People suffering from vertigo or climbing difficulties were advised not to buy seats in this section for the Leeds match, as the lifts were not yet working, but what were the opinions of some of those who ventured into the unknown? *"An excellent view where you can see all the action"* one said, while another thought it was *"too far from the action and would not like to sit there again"*. The majority of opinions, however, gave it the thumbs up.

On Friday April 26th, a giant crane moved onto the Old Trafford forecourt, to manoeuvre an 11ft high bronze statue of Sir Matt Busby onto a podium below the Munich Memorial, on the roof of the entrance into the executive boxes facing Sir Matt Busby Way. The specially commissioned statue, weighing more than one ton, was the work of

The Sir Matt Busby Statue

sculptor Philip Jackson ,and inside the hollow figure were some of the scarves, shirts etc. which had been placed on the forecourt following the great man's death. The following day, a special ceremony was held when members of Sir Matt's family, civic dignitaries and club officials were present at the unveiling.

A ceremony of a different kind took place at the ground a week later, when a Heaton Mersey couple became the first to be married at the stadium, following the club's successful application in February to be able to hold marriage ceremonies. Unfortunately the law did not allow the ceremony to be carried out on the actual pitch, so the Premier Suite was used.

April 27th brought Nottingham Forest to Old Trafford, and a victory would put United within touching distance of the Championship. A crowd of 53,926 were present that afternoon as three vital points were won with a memorable 5-0 victory. Cautious play and a couple of near misses looked

like all the opening half would produce, but Paul Scholes lifted the pressure a little in the 41st minute, stabbing home, before David Beckham added a second 3 minutes later with an opportunist header. The same individual increased the lead 10 minutes into the second half to put the outcome beyond any doubt, and further goals from Giggs and Cantona in the 70th and 90th minutes sent the crowd home dreaming of another title triumph.

The smiles soon disappeared off some of the faces, when it was announced a couple of days later that 2,300 seats in the central section of the new stand would be an executive area the following season, with higher quality catering and parking facilities. Previously priced at £340, the new area would cost a staggering £1,169, preventing most (if not all) of the supporters who sat there - many from its opening in 1965 - from returning to their old places. A further executive area was earmarked for another 1,300 seats in the first 12 rows of the second tier.

A week after the victory over Forest, a 3-0 win at Middlesbrough secured the Championship, while the following Saturday, a late Eric Cantona goal clinched a remarkable 'double-double' with a 1-0 win over Liverpool in the F.A. Cup Final at Wembley, bringing to an end a remarkable season in the club's history.

An almost empty Old Trafford was the venue for an England Vs. Holland under-15 international on May 4th, but attendances would be much different for the forthcoming Euro '96 matches which were beginning to capture the imagination of the public. Groundsman Keith Kent and the other backroom staff had the stadium looking superb, and the introduction of the latest technology from Canada in the form of a germinating blanket for use in the goalmouths, which increased temperatures by 8° to encourage growth, helped towards a perfect playing surface.

Old Trafford had never looked better as the club prepared to entertain thousands of supporters, players, officials and media representatives from abroad. A special media centre had been constructed within the ground for the use of the 300 plus journalists covering the games in Manchester. It was boasted, that the facilities were so good that a journalist could report on the whole of the tournament from this room, without having to watch a game live!

There was also a new facility for the fans, a Midland Bank Cash dispenser. So, if you ran out of cash for your Mega Store purchases or the ticket tout prices were more than you had in your wallet, your immediate problems were now over!

The Championships got under way at Old Trafford on June 9th, with the opening Group C match between Germany and the Czech Republic, watched by 37,300. The eventual winners got off the a perfect start, defeating their opponents in the later Final 2-0. Seven days later they went one better with a 3-0 defeat of Russia in front off 50,760. At one point this match looked like being postponed due to a bomb explosion in central Manchester the previous day, but it went ahead as planned. Sadly the Germans third game in the group failed to produce any goals to satisfy the appetite of the 53,740.

Old Trafford, and Manchester, remained the German's 'home' for the Quarter-Finals, with Croatia narrowly losing 2-1 in front of a somewhat disappointing 43,412.

Slightly over 400 more spectators watched the Semi-Final tie between the Czechs and France, which remained goalless after 90 minutes. Extra time also failed to produce a goal, so it was down to penalties with the Czech team eventually winning 6-5.

As the players made their way off the pitch, Keith Kent and his staff moved into their normal after match routine, but waiting outside the ground was a much larger squad of workers, who were ready to move onto the groundsman's precious patch. Scheduled for Old Trafford on the eve of the Wembley Euro '96 Final was 'The Crowd Are On The Pitch - Euro '96 Extravaganza'. This was a special concert, featuring top Manchester band Simply Red, along with M People, Madness, and Dodgy, with clowns, stiltwalkers and a troupe of acrobats. Normally preparations for such an event took a week, but the 320 workers had only 60 hours to transform the ground. The riggers and roadies worked in 24 hour shifts to complete the job, with 30 trucks bringing the equipment to the stadium.

Around 60,000 flocked to the ground on a fine Manchester night, and on a huge elevated stage in the centre of the pitch, complete with large video screens, United manager Alex Ferguson appeared to open the concert with the words - *"Welcome to the Theatre of Dreams"*, before introducing Simply Red fronted by United fanatic Mick Hucknal.

The unique Old Trafford atmosphere was soon in evidence and the evening turned into something special. The pitch was covered with fans, security and technicians and the support group, M People, soon had everybody in the stadium dancing as they played their hits, with the mood continuing as Simply Red brought a unique evening to a close. Old Trafford had not experienced so much singing and dancing since the Blackburn Rovers match of season 1992-93, following that first title triumph for 26 years.

✛ THE FUTURE? ✛

Many will only see the new North Stand development from their seats inside the ground, or when they take a club tour, but once it has been fitted out, what will the interior contain besides the passageways to seats, toilets and refreshment stalls?

On level one will be a bar dining area, along with part of the new club museum. The main part of the museum will be on level two and will incorporate a classroom and a 112 seater cinema. There will also be another dining area and kitchen.

Level three will also house part of the museum, an executive suite, box-holders lounge and bar, another kitchen and the Red Cafe - a theme restaurant. The final fourth level will provide further dining facilities. So, what will the future hold for the stadium? It is difficult to gauge what level the support will reach if the team continues to be successful as it had been over the past few years, so whether there will be a call for a further increase in seating remains to be seen.

Although it would not be impossible to enlarge the stadium further, either extending out above K Stand, or building over the railway to develop the main stand, it could be considered impractical, with the costs and overall disruptions deterring such moves. Perhaps some consideration could be given to providing the new stadium with a bit of character, which it does seem to lack. The Sir Matt Busby statue and Munich memorials do help along this line, but would a few large club badges on the outside of the ground help in any way?

Will adjoining areas to the ground see something along the lines of a Fred the Red theme park, along with a hotel to generate further income or other United associated ventures? Who knows? At present, however, no matter what day of the week you visit the ground, it is a hive of activity, especially during the schools summer break, when the crowds would be the envy of many lesser clubs' on a Saturday afternoon in mid-season. Old Trafford on a match day is an experience to be savoured and enjoyed, with the area around Chester Road and Sir Matt Busby Way resembling a Middle Eastern Market with the countless traders doing brisk business from early morning. Fast food outlets and an off licence satisfy the hunger and thirst that United cannot supply, while stalls set up by independent traders sell everything from badges to flags and T-shirts, to old match programmes of past seasons. Slightly less audible than the stallholders declaring their wares are the mumbled voices of the ticket touts offering to buy or sell those precious pieces of paper that are required to be admitted to the ground.

As kick-off approaches, Sir Matt Busby Way becomes busier as the legions of far flung supporters make their way over the railway bridge in anticipation of the afternoons fixture. From the city centre the local buses drop their fares along Chester Road while from the opposite direction come the members of the vast red army who have journeyed from all corners of the country in their various supporters club coaches. Many others have arrived in the city by train and have made the short journey to the nearby Old Trafford station adjacent to the cricket ground of the same name, by the Metro Link, a much more modern and quicker method of transport than the trains that would pull up alongside the platform a short pass from the main stand.

All a far cry from the days when a large majority of the supporters were Mancunians and travelled to the match by bicycle, leaving them behind the ground for four old pence.

No matter how you came or how often you come, each visit to Old Trafford is enjoyed and the memories of those visits - the games, the goals, the players, will always be there.

✧✧ Welcome to Old Trafford, The Theatre Of Dreams

Sequence of Major Developments:

1910: Opening of Old Trafford (Stand on Railway side, terracing elsewhere)

1934: United Road side covered.

1938: Corner sections beside Main Stand covered.

1941: Stadium damaged due to German bombs.

1949: Return to Old Trafford following exile to Maine Road.

1954: Main Stand returned to full use.

1957: Floodlights installed.

1959: Stretford End covered.

1965: Cantilever Stand on United Road side opened.

1971: Section of terracing behind Stretford End cleared due to object being thrown.

1972: 'K' Stand opened.

1974: Pitch width fencing erected behind each goal erected (following pitch invasion)

1976: Perimeter fencing extended to completely surround playing area.

1985: Family Stand opened.

1986: Museum opened, and new Floodlights installed on Stand roof.

1989: Perimeter fencing removed.

1990: United Road Paddock converted to seating.

1991: Paddocks in front of Main Stand converted to seating.

1992: Stretford End demolished; dressing rooms and entrance tunnel moved, new Stand built.

1995: United Road Stand demolished and new three tier North Stand built.

✣ THIS IS OLD TRAFFORD ✣
(All references up to end of 1995/96 season)
Notable United Matches:

'Firsts'

Match:	19 February 1910	Vs Liverpool (3-4)	Att. 45,000.
F.A.Cup-tie:	4 February 1911	Vs. Aston Villa (2-1)	Att. 65,101.
F.L. Cup-tie:	26 October 1960	Vs. Exeter City (4-1)	Att. 15,662.
European Cup-tie:	25 April 1957	Vs. Real Madrid (2-2)	Att. 65,000.
United victory:	5 March 1910	Vs. Sheffield Utd. (1-0)	Att. 40,000.
Goal:	Homer (Vs. Liverpool, 19 February 1910)		
Hat-trick:	Picken (scored four) (Vs. Middlesbrough 30 April 1910)		

Highest Attendances

League (1st Division):	27 December 1920	Vs. Aston Villa	Att. 70,504.
League - 2nd Division:	30 November 1976	Vs. Sunderland	Att. 60,585
European Competition:	25 April 1957	Vs. Real Madrid	Att. 65,000.
F.A.Cup:	2 February 1924	Vs. Huddersfield T.	Att. 66,678
League Cup:	17 December 1969	Vs. Manchester City	Att. 63,418
F.A.Youth Cup:	15 April 1959	Vs. Blackburn R.	Att. 35,949 (Semi-Final,2nd leg)
Overall:	25 March 1939 (Wolves Vs. Grimsby F.A.Cup Semi-Final) Att. 76,962.		

Lowest Attendances:

League:	2 September 1931	Vs. Southampton	Att. 3,507.
F.A.Cup:	11 January 1913	Vs. Coventry City	Att. 11,500.

Results - Best

League Victory:	4 March 1995	Vs. Ipswich Town	Score: 9-0.
F.A.Cup Victory:	14 January 1928	Vs. Brentford	Score: 7-1.
League Cup Victory:	27 October 1976	Vs. Newcastle Utd.	Score: 7-2
European Victory:	15 October 1963	Vs. Willem II	Score: 6-1

Results -Worst:

League Defeat:	14 March 1914	Vs. Aston Villa	Score: 0-6
	10 September 1927	Vs. Newcastle Utd.	Score: 1-7
	10 September 1930	Vs. Huddersfield T.	Score: 0-6
F.A.Cup Defeat:	1 February 1961	Vs. Sheffield Wed.	Score: 2-7
League. Cup Defeat:	1 December 1976	Vs. Everton	
	25 October 1989	Vs. Tottenham H.	Score: 0-3
	20 September	Vs. York City	
European Competition:	Never lost a match.		

Appearances and Goals:

Briefest	Paul Wratten 2 April 1991 Vs. Wimbledon 6 minutes.
Youngest player	Jeff Whitefoot 15 April 1950 Vs. Portsmouth 16 years 105 days
Yougest Team:	27 August 1955 Vs. West Bromwich Albion
	Wood, Foulkes, Byrne, Whitefoot, Ives, Edwards, Webster,
	Blanchflower,Lewis, Violett, Scanlon - average 22 years 106 days.

Fastest (United) Goal:	Ryan Giggs Vs. Southampton (September 1995)	15 seconds.
Most Goals in a game:	Andy Cole Vs. Ipswich Town (March 1995)	5 goals.

Other (Non-Manchester United) Notable Matches:

F.A.Cup Final:

1911	Bradford City	Vs. Newcastle Utd.	(1-0) - Replay.
1915	Sheffield United	Vs. Chelsea	(3-0).
1970	Chelsea	Vs. Leeds United	(2-1 after extra time) - Replay.

F.A.Cup Semi-Final:

1910	Barnsley	Vs. Everton	(3-0) - Replay.
1914	Sheffield United	Vs. Burnley	(0-0)
1921	Wolverhampton W.	Vs. Cardiff C.	(3-1) - Replay
1923	Bolton Wand.	Vs. Sheffield Wed.	(1-0)
1928	Huddersfield T.	Vs. Sheffield Utd.	(2-2)
1930	Huddersfield T.	Vs. Sheffield Wed.	(2-1)
1931	Everton	Vs. West Brom. Alb.	(0-1)
1939	Wolverhampton W.	Vs. Grimsby Town	(5-0)
1968	Everton	Vs. Leeds United	(1-0)
1971	Everton	Vs. Liverpool	(1-2)
1972	Arsenal	Vs. Stoke City	(2-1)
1974	Leicester City	Vs. Liverpool	(0-0) *
1989	Liverpool	Vs. Nottingham F.	(3-1)
1996	Liverpool	Vs. Aston Villa	(3-0)

* Record (at that time) receipts at Old Trafford taken - £104,000.

F.A.Charity Shield (non-Manchester United match):

| 1928 | Everton | Vs. Blackburn Rovers. |

Football League Cup Final:

| 1977 | Aston Villa | Vs. Everton - 2nd Replay |
| 1978 | Liverpool | Vs. Nottingham F. - Replay |

Football League Cup Semi-Final:

| 1961 | Aston Villa | Vs. Burnley - Replay. |
| 1972 | Stoke City | Vs. West Ham United - 2nd Replay. |

Post-War F.A. Cup-Ties (Replay):

1955	Bury	Vs. Stoke City (3rd round, 4th replay)
1958	Rochdale	Vs. Hartlepool United (1st round, 2nd replay)
1962	Liverpool	Vs. Preston North End (5th round, 2nd replay)
1964	Barrow	Vs. Grimsby Town (1st round, 2nd replay)
1969	Wigan Athletic	Vs. Port Vale (1st round, 2nd replay)
1970	Barnsley	Vs. Rhyl (2nd round, 2nd replay)
1971	Stoke City	Vs. Huddersfield Town (4th round, 2nd replay)
1975	Altrincham	Vs. Everton (3rd round, replay)

League/Milk Cup (Replay)

1973	Manchester City	Vs. Walsall (2nd round, 2nd replay)
1977	Manchester City	Vs. Luton Town (3rd round, 2nd replay)
1985	Bury	Vs. Manchester City (2nd round, 1st leg)

Full International:

1926 (April 17)	England Vs. Scotland (0-1)	
1938 (November 16)	England Vs. Ireland	
1966 (July 13)	Hungary Vs. Portugal (1-3)	World Cup.
1966 (July 16)	Portugal Vs. Bulgaria (3-0)	World Cup.
1966 (July 20)	Hungary Vs. Bulgaria (3-1)	World Cup.
1991 (May 28)	Argentina Vs. Russia - English Challenge Cup.	
1996 (June 9)	Germany Vs. Czech. Republic (2-0)	Euro '96
1996 (June 16)	Russia Vs. Germany (0-3)	Euro '96
1996 (June 19)	Italy Vs. Germany (0-0)	Euro '96
1996 (June 23)	Germany Vs. Croatia (2-1)	Euro '96
1996 (June 26)	France Vs. Czech Rep. (0-0, 5-6 pens.)	Euro '96

Under-23 International:

1963 (March 21)	England Vs. Yugoslavia
1969 (October 22)	England Vs. Russia
1976 (March 23)	England Vs. Hungary

Inter-League:

1961 (November 8)	Football League Vs. Italian League

Miscellaneous:

1912-13	Football League Vs Southern League
1917	Manchester XI Vs. Belgian Army XI
1984-85	Celtic Vs. Rapid Vienna (E.C.W.C.)

(Other Representative games include: F.A.XI Vs. Army 1957-58, F.A.XI Vs. R.A.F. 1960-61, England Youth and Schoolboy [various], England Vs. Norway (Women) 1990-91)

Post-War Minor Internationals and Principal Representative Matches:

1946-47:	Salford Boys Vs. Leicester Boys (English Schools Final Replay)
1947-48:	England Vs. Ireland (Schoolboy International)
1948-49:	Manchester Boys Vs. Liverpool Boys (English Schools Shield 6th round)
1949-50:	Manchester Boys Vs. South Northumberland Boys (English Schools Shield 6th rd.rep.)
1051-52:	Salford Boys Vs. Manchester Boys (Lancs. Schools Cup Final 2nd leg)
1951-52	Collegiate Old Boys Vs. Manchester University (Lancs.Amateur Cup Final)
1956-57:	England Vs. The Rest (English Schools International Trial)
1958-59:	Lancs. Boys Vs. Cheshire Boys (Lancs Schools Inter-County Match)
1959-60:	Lancs. FA Vs. Cheshire FA (FA County Youth Challenge, 1st round)
1959-60:	Manchester County FA Vs. Lancs. County FA (FA County Youth Challenge, 2nd rd.)
1961-62:	Lancs.Boys Vs. Birmingham & District (Lancs. Schools FA Inter-County Match)
1963-64:	Rusholme Vs. Quarry Bank Old Boys (Lancs. Amateur Cup Final)
1966-67:	England Vs. Scotland (Schoolboy International Victory Shield)
1966-67:	Stretford Vs. Middleston ((Stretford & District Secondary Schools FA Final)
1969-70:	Lancs SFA Vs. English SFA (Lancs. Schools FA Jubilee Match)
1973-74:	England Vs. Scotland (Schoolboy International)
1976-77:	England Vs. Scotland (Schoolboy International Victory Shield)
1980-81:	England Vs. Scotland (Schoolboy International)
1982-83:	Sweden Vs. Czechoslovakia (European Youth Championship)
1986-87:	Blackburn & Darwen Vs. Sefton (English Schools FA Granada Cup Final U-14's)
1987-88:	Salford Vs. Belfast (Salford Schools FA Sir Matt Busby Challenge Match)
1988-89:	England Vs. Scotland (Schoolboy International Victory Shield)
1988-89:	Salford Schools Vs. St. Helens Schools
1988-89:	Salford Schools Vs. Plymouth Schools (English Schools FA Trophy Semi-Final)
1989-90:	Salford City Vs. Curzon Ashton (Manchester County FA Premiership Final)
1995-96:	England Vs. Holland (Schoolboy International)

1928

1914: F.A.Cup Final crowd (The 'Khaki Final')

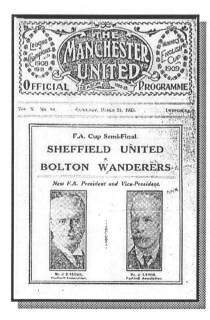

1923 **1926** **1930**

1938

MANCHESTER UNITED
FOOTBALL CLUB LIMITED

Official Programme

Price **1d.**

F.A. Cup 3rd Round—4th Replay

Bury

v.

Stoke City

Monday, 24th January, 1955

1955

1939

1964

1966

1974

Seasonal Average Attendances

(Pre-1909-10 at former grounds. 1909-10 season only part season at old Trafford):

1909-10	18740	1938-39	30365	1970-71	43945
1910-11	24190	(Second World War)		1971-72	45999
1911-12	19040	1946-47	43945#	1972-73	48623 **
1912-13	23610	1947-48	54890#	1973-74	42712 **
1913-14	25515	1948-49	48808#	1974-75	48389 * ††
1914-15	11950	1949-50	43282	1975-76	54750 **
(First World War)		1950-51	39008	1976-77	53710 **
1919-20	26540	1951-52	42916	1977-78	51860 **
1920-21	35525	1952-53	37571	1978-79	46430 **
1921-22	28510	1953-54	36887	1979-80	51608 **
1922-23	22955 *	1954-55	36911	1980-81	45071 **
1923-24	21125 *	1955-56	39254	1981-82	44571 **
1924-25	27995	1956-57	45481 **	1982-83	41695 **
1925-26	27647	1957-58	46073 **	1983-84	42534 **
1926-27	26138	1958-59	53258 **	1984-85	42881 **
1927-28	25555	1959-60	47288	1985-86	46321 **
1928-29	23659	1960-61	37888	1986-87	40594 **
1929-30	18599	1961-62	33491	1987-88	39152
1930-31	11685	1962-63	40329	1988-89	36488
1931-32	13011	1963-64	44125	1989-90	39077 **
1932-33	20149	1964-65	46521 **	1990-91	43218 **
1933-34	18338	1965-66	38769	1991-92	44984 **
1934-35	22871	1966-67	53854 **	1992-93	35132
1935-36	26070	1967-68	57552 ** †	1993-94	44244 **
1936-37	32332	1968-69	51169 **	1994-95	43682 **
1937-38	26633	1969-70	49862 **	1995-96	41681 **

*   Highest Second Division Club Attendance.   **   Highest Overall Club Attendance (First Division)
** † Highest all-time Attendance of any Club   ** †† Highest Overall Club Attendance (Second Division)
#   Home matches played at Maine Road

Ground Capacities (1996-97 season) North Stand 26,084; South Stand 10,183; East Stand 9,802;
West Stand 10,398; **Total: 56,467** (In addition the Executive Boxes have a toal capacity of 1,183)

Other Major Events Staged at Old Trafford

First World War	**Baseball**	(Teams from U.S.A.)
1924-25:	**Rugby League**	(Lancashire Vs. All Blacks)
1925, 1926:	**Athletics Meeting**	(Manchester County Police Annual Sports)
1927:	**Tennis**	(Exhibition by Wimbledon Champ. Suzanne Lenglen)
1958:	**Rugby League**	(Salford Vs. Leeds)
1981:	**Cricket**	(Lambert & Butler Cup)
1986:	**Rugby League**	(Great Britain Vs. Australia Test match)
1987, 1988, 1989:	**Rugby League**	(Premiership Finals)
1989:	**Rugby League**	(Widnes Vs. Canberra Raiders - World Club Champs.)
1989:	**Rugby League**	(Great Britain Vs. New Zealand - Test Match)
1990:	**Rugby League**	(St.Helens Vs.Wigan - Rugby Lge.Chall. Cup Semi-F.)
1990:	**Rugby League**	(Premiership Final)
1990:	**Rugby League**	(Great Britain Vs. Australia - Test Match)
1991:	**Rock Concert**	('Rod Stewart','Status Quo', 'Joe Cocker')
1992 - 1995 incl.	**Rugby League**	(Premiership Finals)
1993:	**Professional Boxing**	(World Super Middleweight Championship)
1994:	**Memorial Service**	(Sir Matt Busby)
1994:	**Religious Service**	(B.B.C.TV 'Songs Of Praise')
1995:	**Rugby League**	(England Vs.Wales-Halifax Centenary World Cup S.Final)
1996:	**Rock Concert**	('Simply Red', 'M People', ' Dodgy')
1996:	**Marriage Ceremony**	(February - in the Premier Suite)

In addition the ground has been used in the production of Films (Cinema and TV), plus advertisements.

- A Selection of Other Major Events -

1958

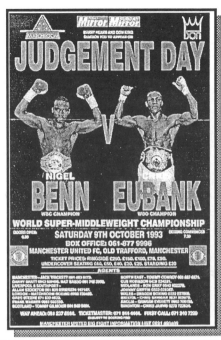

1993

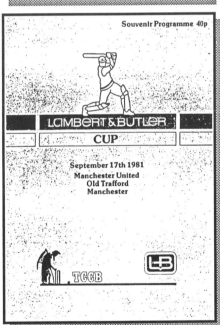

1981

1991

1994

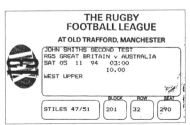

1994

1996

'YORE PUBLICATIONS'
12 The Furrows, Harefield, Middx. UB9 6AT

✦ ✦ ✦ ✦ ✦ ✦ ✦ ✦ ✦ ✦ ✦

(Free lists issued 3 times per year. For your first list please send a S.A.E.) Current titles include:

WYCOMBE WANDERERS - The Official History (1887 - 1996) (Dave Finch & Steve Peart) A very complete history of a club who until a few years ago were in non-League football. Abbreviated statistics from the first game in 1887 (versus Wycombe Nose Club!), to the end of the 1995/96 season (full stats. from 1963/64). In addition to the full written history - plus illustrations (including many team groups), other chapters include 'The Grounds', 'Great Games' and Who's Whos' of League and non-League (from 1963) players. 256 large page hardback, price £16-95 plus £3-80 P/P.

NOTTS COUNTY- The Official History (1862 - 1995) (Tony Brown) The Author, a prominent member of the Association of Football Statisticians, has put together the detailed history of his local club - the oldest team in the Football League. Statistics commence, including line-ups, from 1864 (all **18** players for the first game!), and other sections provide the full well illustrated written history (with a concentration on the early days), named team groups (every season from 1898/99), a Who's Who, plus a most interesting 'A-Z' of the Club: 272 large page hardback, price £16-95 plus £3-80 P/P.

> **Other Club histories include**: Kilmarnock, Bristol City, Southend United, Maidstone United, Doncaster Rovers, Shrewsbury Town, Carlisle United & Colchester United.

TOMMY TAYLOR OF MANCHESTER UNITED AND BARNSLEY (John Kennedy) An excellent biography of this young clubman and international who was one of the victims of the Munich tragedy. The book provides an excellent insight into the player gleaned from interviews with family, friends, and other football personalities. This 84 large page book is well illustrated, with many photographs not published before.

❖❖ A **must** for all United fans, and inexpensively priced at only £6-95 plus 95p P/P. ❖❖

FORGOTTEN CAPS (England Football Internationals of two World Wars) (Bryan Horsnell & Douglas Lamming) A much acclaimed book written by the two leading authorities on the subject. A complete Who's Who record of every England player (including non playing reserves) - over 100. Includes biographies and photographs of **every** player; plus much more, a truly complete record! 112 large pages, price £8-95 plus 85p P/P.

REJECTED F.C. VOLUMES 2 and 3 (Reprints) (Dave Twydell) The Histories of the ex-Football League Clubs (Volume I - reprint - now sold out). Clubs consist: Accrington/Acc. Stanley, Barrow, Darwen, Merthyr Town, Thames Assoc. plus Leeds City (Volume 2), and Durham City, Gainsborough Trin., Middlesbrough Ironopolis, New Brighton/New Brighton Tower, Northwich Vics., Southport plus Wigan Boro' (Volume 3). Each 256 pages (hardback), and priced £12-95 (per copy), plus £1-55 P/P for each volume.

FOOTBALL LEAGUE - GROUNDS FOR A CHANGE (By Dave Twydell). Published 1991. A 424 page, A5 sized, Hardback book. A comprehensive study of all the Grounds on which the current English Football League clubs previously played. Incl. 250 illustrations, with plenty of reading. Price £13-95 Plus £1-75 P/P.

SIMPLY THE BEST (David Ross) 'The Greatest hour-and-a-half of every Football League and Scottish League Club 132 well written stories of each club's greatest match. Well illustrated large pages, price £9-75 plus £1-15 P/P.

Non-League football is also covered, including the 'Gone But Not Forgotten' series (histories of defunct non-League clubs and grounds). Plus the unusual , e.g. 'The Little Red Book of Chinese Football', etc.